THE EDWARDIANS

This book is dedicated to my Edwardian ancestors, the Rippons and the Rowleys, who embodied the entrepreneurial spirit of the new age.

THE EDWARDIANS
LIFE AND TIMES OF THE GOLDEN AGE

NICOLA RIPPON

PEN & SWORD
HISTORY

AN IMPRINT OF PEN & SWORD BOOKS LTD.
YORKSHIRE – PHILADELPHIA

First published in Great Britain in 2025 by
PEN AND SWORD HISTORY
An imprint of
Pen & Sword Books Ltd
Yorkshire – Philadelphia

Copyright © Nicola Rippon, 2025

ISBN 978 1 03610 592 1

The right of Nicola Rippon to be identified as Author of this work has been asserted by her in accordance with the Copyright, Designs and Patents Act 1988.

A CIP catalogue record for this book is available from the British Library.

All rights reserved. No part of this book may be reproduced, transmitted, downloaded, decompiled or reverse engineered in any form or by any means, electronic or mechanical including photocopying, recording or by any information storage and retrieval system, without permission from the Publisher in writing. NO AI TRAINING: Without in any way limiting the Author's and Publisher's exclusive rights under copyright, any use of this publication to "train" generative artificial intelligence (AI) technologies to generate text is expressly prohibited. The Author and Publisher reserve all rights to license uses of this work for generative AI training and development of machine learning language models.

Typeset in Times New Roman 11.5/15 by
SJmagic DESIGN SERVICES, India.
Printed and bound in the UK by CPI Group (UK) Ltd.

The Publisher's authorised representative in the EU for product safety is Authorised Rep Compliance Ltd., Ground Floor, 71 Lower Baggot Street, Dublin D02 P593, Ireland.
www.arccompliance.com

For a complete list of Pen & Sword titles please contact
PEN & SWORD BOOKS LIMITED
George House, Units 12 & 13, Beevor Street, Off Pontefract Road,
Barnsley, South Yorkshire, S71 1HN, England
E-mail: enquiries@pen-and-sword.co.uk
Website: www.pen-and-sword.co.uk

or

PEN AND SWORD BOOKS
1950 Lawrence Rd, Havertown, PA 19083, USA
E-mail: uspen-and-sword@casematepublishers.com
Website: www.penandswordbooks.com

Contents

Introduction vi

Chapter 1   Sombre Clad … 1
Chapter 2   Greater Britain Overseas … 8
Chapter 3   A Background of Slaughter 24
Chapter 4   Vivat Rex! 35
Chapter 5   Establishing Modern Britain 47
Chapter 6   Broken Bones Better Than Broken Promises 56
Chapter 7   Crimes and Punishment 80
Chapter 8   Deplorable Sacrifices of Human Life 87
Chapter 9   Upstairs, Downstairs – The Edwardians at Home 104
Chapter 10   The Gentle Art of Beauty, the Conceits of Fashion ... 119
Chapter 11   The Battle of Shepherd's Bush 134
Chapter 12   Down at the Old Bull and Bush 146
Chapter 13   Oh, I Do Like To Be Beside The Seaside 161
Chapter 14   The Holly and the Ivy 169
Chapter 15   Death of the Peacemaker King 174
Chapter 16   The Last Summer 183

Index 188

Introduction

The great Edwardian Age was short-lived. Technically speaking it lasted less than a decade but, in practical terms, continued on until a world war brought it to a sudden close.

When we think of Edwardian Britain, we often imagine Edwardian Britons as grandiose men and women, bedecked in their finery and with imposing homes and lavish lifestyles. It was the so-called 'Golden Age'. People living in a country bound by centuries of tradition, and very different from what we know today.

At the beginning of Edward VII's reign in 1901, Britain was an economically and militarily global power. In part, its strength lay in its evolving relationship with its colonies. Slavery had been ended in the British Empire in the very early months of Queen Victoria's reign, yet still Britain controlled more than one-fifth of the globe. It enjoyed alliances with several of its European neighbours – alliances that would eventually lead Britain along a path to a devastating war.

And yet, so much of what we experience today has its roots in the Edwardian Age. Everyday life was changing at speed. A more enlightened society would see improvements in the welfare of everyone, and a new, aspirational, class.

A technological age was dawning. The increasingly widespread use of electricity would soon prove both a wonder and a necessity. Improvements in transportation would mean our Edwardian forebears could travel from one end of the country to the other in a matter of hours, rather than days. They could now travel for work, or leisure, and back again with relative ease.

Introduction

People from all walks of life, and those from different parts of the country, and even different lands, encountered one another as never before. The early telegraph, telegram and telephone systems would eventually become a telecommunications revolution.

Sandwiched between the great Victorian Age and the First World War, the Edwardian Age stands out as the moment at which an embryonic modern Britain began.

Nicola Rippon
February 2025

CHAPTER 1

SOMBRE CLAD ...

Her Majesty declared to be in extremis. Sands of Life Rapidly Running Out. Completeness of the breakdown. Immediate nearness of the end.
>Sheffield and Rotherham Independent,
>21 January 1901

On 21 January 1901, Britons read the news that no one had expected: Queen Victoria, their monarch for sixty-three years, was nearing the end of her life.

Now 81 and suffering from rheumatism, and cataracts in both eyes, which limited her participation in public life, the Queen's health had been in decline for some years. Yet she had been blessed with a sturdy constitution – and seemingly remarkable powers of recovery. Four years earlier she had even survived a French newspaper report that she had been dead for eighteen years, her public appearances being fulfilled by a humble lookalike. So the headlines were a shock to the nation. Age-related conditions and European false news aside, there had been little to suggest that Victoria was ailing to the extent that the public was now being told.

Victoria was Britain's longest-reigning monarch, the only monarch most people had known. Now the woman who had become the very definition of six decades of British life, in many ways the nation's guiding force, an example to everyone, was nearing her end.

Any hope that the Queen might recover, as she had so many times before, was put to rest with the news that all public engagements by the royal family had been cancelled, and that members of the Cabinet had been told not to travel far from London. Newspapers did not sugar-coat the news. The *Sheffield and Rotherham Independent* reflected that 'it's been well said that the Queen has been sovereign so long – she was on the throne when most of us were born – that she is coming to be looked upon as immortal'. But now, although 'there is belief in Court physician circles that the Queen may survive some time', for sovereign purposes she would be 'incompetent'. The Victorian Era was all but over.

Accompanied by siblings, nephews and nieces, Victoria's son, the 59-year-old Prince of Wales, known to the family as 'Bertie', now made his way to the Isle of Wight where his mother had recently spent much of her time, on the north of the island at Osborne House, designed by her husband, Prince Albert, as a summer holiday retreat for the family. Making the hurried journey from the Continent were another son, Arthur, the Duke of Connaught, and her grandson, Kaiser Wilhelm II of Germany.

Victoria died at 6.30pm the following day, in her sleep, peacefully and painlessly, her close family at her bedside. Immediately an official bulletin was released. The evening editions of local newspapers broke the news in their stop press columns: 'Prince Wales telegraphs Lord Mayor ... My beloved mother the Queen just passed away surrounded by her children.'

Within minutes of the Lord Mayor of London receiving the telegram, 'Great Paul', the largest of St Paul's Cathedral's four bells, began to toll once every minute for the next two hours. Soon the peals were joined by the voices of newsboys on London's streets. 'The Queen is Dead!' they cried.

The Daily News, founded by Charles Dickens, described the unfolding scene:

> Everyone seems dazed with the shock ... Every kind of traffic and movement stopped dead for a few moments ... everyone seemed stunned ... the doors of the theatres were closing ... shopkeepers hastily took in their goods and put up their shutters. The streets fluttered from end to end with papers. The public grief, lacking any public

method of expression, was dumb, and showed itself only in the scared faces of the crowds as they passed. Groups of passers-by, perfect strangers to each other, were drawn into familiarity by this overwhelming sorrow, and spoke of the sad significance of the event in low voices. At almost every large establishment or semi-public office the news was posted up and read by an awestruck gathering. It was a time of gloom heavy and unrelieved.

Tens of thousands of Londoners were still returning home on trams and buses and on railway trains. The news spread from one commuter to another so that by that evening it had reached the furthest edges of a metropolis that was home to five million people.

In Britain, a mood of mourning and grief would soon pervade every town, city, and village. *The Derby Daily Telegraph* summed up: 'The nation's sorrow in the face of its great loss is absolutely without precedent. The blow, indeed, is rendered all the heavier because of the suddenness with which it has descended.'

Victoria's subjects, in the most distant corners of her empire, learned of her death thanks to the latest technological advances of the telegraph. Of course, it was no longer Victoria's empire. As soon as a British monarch draws their last breath, their successor begins to reign. Britons looked to their new king who, although christened Albert Edward, had chosen Edward VII as his regnal name, leaving his late father's name to stand alone in the story of the British monarchy.

The new king had immediate constitutional duties to perform. The following morning Edward VII, together with the Duke of Connaught, the Duke of York, the Lord Chamberlain (Edward Hyde Villiers, 5th Earl of Clarendon) and Arthur Balfour MP, who had been at Osborne House representing the Prime Minister, his uncle the Marquess of Salisbury, returned to London for meetings with the Privy Council and with Parliament.

The Western Echo described the scene to its readers:

> To his subjects who watched in silence his coming it was, as it must have been to himself, an advent of solemn

significance. They thronged the approaches to his palace. Sombre clad with countenances of preoccupied seriousness, and with voices that communicated their thoughts only in undertone, they sought to demonstrate by their presence and mute figures the interest they felt in the occasion and the sympathy that filled every heart ... they could not actually see their king, for he sat back in a corner of his closed carriage, but he could not fail to see them, and he must have been touched with the aspect of his people – if his mind could yet be diverted from the bereavement with which he has just been stricken. The British constitution left him, indeed, little leisure for indulgence and grief. Its call upon him to attend the office of state was urgent and imperative. His Privy Council awaited his presence, countless orders could only emanate from him had yet to be given to prevent a sudden stoppage of the executive and administrative machinery of the nation. His ministers, judges, and other functionaries had, by a fresh oath of allegiance, to renew their title to government, judgement, and direction. Parliament, now become his, was about to assemble and acknowledge their new sovereign. Everything, in short, awaited his word, and it was a sense of the importance of all this that allowed the inhabitants of the capital to make it evident that they realised the onerous nature of his obligations and duties, and that they wished him well in the faithful discharge of them.

That evening Edward returned to Osborne as preparations for his mother's funeral were put in place. It might have been decades since the funeral of a British monarch, but Victoria had meticulously planned hers, requesting that she – as the daughter of a solider and head of the armed forces – be given a military funeral.

She had also set out certain personal requests and conditions. Reputedly, her personal physician, Sir James Reid, saw to it that a number of sentimental items were placed inside her coffin. A plaster cast of the hand of her beloved Albert, together with his wedding ring

Sombre Clad ...

and dressing gown. A cape made for Albert by their late daughter, Alice. A photograph and lock of hair of her dear friend and personal attendant John Brown, and a ring, once Brown's mother's wedding band, that he had given to Victoria. There, too, was a small bouquet of Scottish heather. The Queen, who had worn black every day of her forty-eight-year widowhood, was dressed in a white gown and her wedding veil.

On Friday, 1 February 1901, thousands of locals lined the streets of the island as Victoria's coffin was taken from Osborne House upon a gun carriage to Trinity Pier at East Cowes where HMY *Alberta*, the tender to the larger Royal Yacht *Victoria and Albert*, awaited. The *Alberta* carried Victoria across the Solent into Gosport, escorted by two columns of destroyers. It was followed by the Royal Family aboard the *Victoria and Albert* and the night was spent aboard before the entire party transferred to Portsmouth railway station and on to London. Arriving at the station which bore her name, Victoria was again borne on a gun carriage to Paddington station, before continuing to Windsor.

As Victoria had decreed, there would be no public lying-in-state; the journey through the streets of the capital was the only opportunity for her subjects to pay personal homage to their late queen. In London, crowds had begun to gather early on a bitterly cold and wet day. Pavements were crowded even before the early-morning milk carts rattled by on their rounds. On Edgeware Road, women laid down rugs over the pavement edges, cradling the day's provisions, and studying the morning newspaper for details of what was to pass. There were similar scenes in Piccadilly, at Hyde Park and Green Park, along St James's, and outside Buckingham Palace, too. With daylight came more and more people. At Victoria station where, according to *The Daily News*, the people were 'vomiting forth', crowds were prevented from walking on a spotless length of violet carpet, guarded by policemen ready for the royal arrivals. At Marble Arch, the Tube became so busy that the staircase was blocked.

According to *The Daily News*,

> North to south on the Park Lane and the western side the people were banked up in an unbroken mass, a very

continent of humanity, and every minute until the expected moment arrived the broad belt of black widened westward, until the whole space to the furthest trees seemed carpeted with people, and every tree that offered the least chance of foothold was festooned with spectators.

The reporter noted that those present represented 'the real London ... the London which nurses no conventional sentiment at its heart and speaks in Cockney accents, which can work itself into delirium under strong excitement, or stand to the world, as it did on Saturday, for the very embodiment of a national sentiment.'

The majority were 'youngish and middle-aged', and the mood was not entirely mournful. The crowd chatted, many finding it hard not to refer to Edward as 'the Prince of Wales', and discussing the other royals and people of note. As the coffin approached, the mood changed and a respectful silence fell upon the scene. For two hours the cortege wound its way slowly between the two railway stations.

Across the country the day was dedicated to mourning. *The Daily News* again:

> Throughout the entire Kingdom, Saturday was observed as one of national mourning. The whole population wore mourning, more or less deep; in every town and village the shops, offices, and public houses were closed; on many railways trains were run as on Sundays; blinds were generally drawn, and public buildings were draped; and memorial services were held in the Cathedrals and in all Anglican churches.

From Aberdeen and Aberystwyth to Worcester and York, there was the same air of solemnity.

Back at Windsor station, the procession was about to set out for St George's Chapel when there was a problem with the gun carriage. Accounts vary; one has it that the horses reared up and it was feared that they would topple the carriage; another is that, as the horses moved off, an eyelet on the splinter bar of the gun carriage broke. Whatever happened there was little option but to deploy the naval guard of honour, who pulled the carriage through the town to the chapel – beginning a tradition followed at monarchs' funerals to this day. Decades later, one of Victoria's grandchildren who witnessed the funeral, Princess Alice, Countess of Athlone, said, 'It was better, it looked beautiful, but, of course, the artillery were furious, you can imagine. Humiliated beyond words.'

On Monday, 4 February, after two days of a private lying-in-state in the Albert Memorial Chapel, Victoria's coffin was taken to the Royal Mausoleum at Frogmore, where the late queen was buried alongside her husband.

The Victorian Age had come to an end. It was time for Edward VII, then the longest-waiting heir to a British throne, to step forward as ruler of the United Kingdom and many lands far beyond.

The Golden Age had begun.

CHAPTER 2

GREATER BRITAIN OVERSEAS ...

> When we gain new territories, we open them to the trade of the world. This is why it is in the interests of the whole world that the British Empire should continue to expand.
> Belfast News-Letter, 1901

Edward VII inherited an empire that was, perhaps, at its proudest. It extended to more than ten million square miles – more than one-fifth of the planet – as the tentacles of British imperial control touched vast swathes of five continents, influencing the lives of more than 400 million people.

It was no coincidence that in the summer of 1901, at the recently founded Proms concerts, composer Edward Elgar had debuted his then instrumental *Pomp and Circumstance March No 1*. The following year he wrote the stirring lyrics to *Land of Hope and Glory*, and the two elements were performed together at the last concert of the Proms of 1905, and at the first and last concerts of the 1909 season.

In 1906, the government issued a 'Blue Book' detailing a snapshot of the Empire taken in 1901, to coincide with the British census of the same year. With Great Britain covering only 121,039 square miles, acquisitions in Africa and Asia over the previous forty years had increased the Empire's size by a remarkable 40 per cent to an estimated 11,908,378 square miles. By far the largest portion of this was in Asia, with more than 300 million residents. India and Bengal (making up modern India, Pakistan and Bangladesh) were the largest, but Hong Kong, Borneo, Burma (Myanmar), Malaya (Malaysia), Siam (Thailand) and the Spice Islands (Maluku Islands) were also under British control.

The Blue Book divided residents into two groups. 'White' consisted of only 13.6 per cent, the huge majority being classified 'Coloured'. In terms of population density, only the Isle of Man and the Channel Islands (at 496.3 people per square mile) exceeded the United Kingdom's 342.4. The vastness of British 'possessions' in Asia was responsible for its relative spaciousness of just 161.7 people per square mile. Australasia came in at only 1.6.

There were 187 Empire cities and towns that boasted populations of above 50,000, eighty-seven of which were in the United Kingdom. There were seventy-eight in India, where one-third of the population was engaged in agricultural work.

Religiously speaking the Empire was 'roughly divided into five main groups'. These were Hindus – by far the largest with more than 200 million adherents; 94 million Mohammedans – as Muslims were then known; 58 million Christians; 12 million Buddhists; and 23 million others from 'Primitive Animistic, Pagan and other non-Christian religions'.

According to the *Birmingham Gazette & Express*, recording the very many 'weird religions' observed across the Empire proved problematic. 'Strange sects' had been listed, many of which, like Ambrosians and Antinomians, were little-known derivatives of Christianity.

'Infirmity' was also recorded. The United Kingdom and Malta apparently had the greatest percentage of 'lunatics and imbeciles', which said a great deal about the way in which Britain and its Empire chose to regard citizens with mental health conditions or intellectual disabilities.

This was the first time a census of sorts had been completed for the entire Empire, although methods, and even questions, had varied from territory to territory. And, in some of the parts that proved difficult to reach, methodical research had been replaced by estimates.

Despite the obvious challenges, it was decided that the census had been a success and that, preferably before the next one in 1911, some kind of uniformity be designed for use across the Empire.

For the most part Britain, like the Dutch and Spanish, had expanded its Empire as a business. The establishment of various mercantile companies, which controlled colonies and trade, sought to provide Britain with a steady and guaranteed supply of raw materials and produce, as well as ready export markets for finished goods. Nigeria, which had been effectively under British control since the mid-1800s, was established as a single country in 1914 when the British Protectorates of Northern and Southern Nigeria – until 1900 controlled by the Royal Niger Company on behalf of Britain – were combined.

The very nature of the Empire, and the way in which it had been colonised, meant that there was often great diversity in how the colonies were run, even within a relatively local area. The six British colonies of Australia had their own discrete laws, tariffs, and even railway gauges. On 1 January 1901, six of the British colonies in Australasia had become legally federated into one country – known as the Commonwealth of Australia, with the New Zealand colony opting not to join, instead becoming a dominion in its own right in 1907.

More and more colonies were coming under direct Crown rule and, in 1902, a conference agreed either reciprocal tariffs or free-trade arrangements between the Dominions and Colonies. The United Kingdom itself, however, was subject to its own free-trade commitments and was unable to comply with the agreement.

In 1904, a Government white paper revealed that most of the British colonies favoured the idea of using the metric measurement over the Imperial system. Serious discussions about adopting the metric system in Britain itself had taken place in 1818, but it had instead been decided to regulate the existing Imperial system. In 1896 Parliament passed the Weights and Measures (Metric System) Act, legalising the use of metric units, but not making them compulsory – essentially beginning the duality that remains in Britain to this day, despite the metrication and decimalisation of various elements.

Although his coronation had taken place at Westminster Abbey in August 1902, and Edward VII had automatically assumed the title of Emperor of India, an official ceremony was held in Delhi to mark his accession. Other Imperial Durbars (from the Persian word for 'court') held – in 1877 for Victoria and 1911 for George V – were grand enough affairs. But that which Lord Curzon, Viceroy of India, designed for Edward VII was far more elaborate and spectacular. Staged between December 1902 and 10 January 1903, it took place five miles north of Delhi where a huge, tented city was built. It had full electricity and sophisticated sanitation. There was a temporary light railway to bring spectators out from Delhi, although 'every conceivable sort of conveyance was requisitioned'. A dedicated police force with its own uniform, a hospital, a magistrates' court, shops of all kinds, and even a post office, telephone and telegraph office were created. The complex was so big that official guidebooks and maps were sold. The King himself did not attend, instead his brother, Prince Arthur, the Duke of Connaught, was guest of honour. An estimated 15,000 subjects attended in person.

A report in the *Western Mail* described it thus: 'The Emperor of India. Proclamation Durbar at Delhi. Scene of unparalleled magnificence ... The event was characterised by a great spectacular display and by an imposing demonstration of loyalty to the British Crown on the part of the representatives of the Indian nations.'

There was no shortage of visual detail for British newspaper readers to consume, from the splendour of the uniforms and ladies' outfits, to all the colour and sound of the ceremony, the parades and entertainment. The *Western Mail* again:

> The Durbar is over, and words fail to convey across the seas an adequate impression of its sublime splendour. Waves of movement of colour and of sound are the only general terms in which one can express the effects produced upon the mind ... Some approach to reality may be reached by those who can imagine the most brilliant spectacle ever presented upon a stage magnified hundred-fold.

Of course, not all of those 400 million citizens of the British Empire wished to be part of it. Throughout Victoria's reign there had been various uprisings – on the Indian subcontinent and in Africa in particular, but also in other parts of Asia, and in New Zealand and the West Indies.

Apart from the occasional news item, in Britain itself little attention was paid to any of them, including the Indian independence movement. In 1909, however, an act of violence on home soil forced it into the public consciousness. It took place at London's Imperial Institute where the Indian National Association was holding its annual 'At Home' function. The association's aim was to promote social interaction between Britons and Indians living in London. Madan Lal Dhingra, who had just finished his studies at the University College, had been invited to the event by Emma Beck, the association's honorary secretary. She told the *Daily Telegraph* that Dhingra was just one of around 200 Indian students, and a large number of Britons at the event. Dhingra was closely involved with the Abhinav Bharat Society, a militant group working towards independence. Earlier in the year he had planned to kill Lord Curzon, and Bampfylde Fuller, the former Lieutenant-Governor of East Bengal, but turned his attention towards Sir Curzon Wyllie, a political aide-de-camp to the Secretary of State for India who, as treasurer to the association, attended more public events and who had some connections with Dhingra's wider family.

Emma Beck said:

> It was eleven o'clock, and over half the guests had left the hall when shots rang out. It was said there were six, but the reports seemed as if they would never come to an end. We did not know what had happened, but the news soon spread that Sir Curzon Wyllie had been shot. The Indian student had been in the reception room the whole evening, and only a short time before had been telling my sister about his examination. He waited in the vestibule ... the shots rang out as soon as he [Sir Curzon] got into the vestibule. I believe the student's actions were premeditated.

Sir Curzon had been shot four times in the head and was pronounced dead at the scene.

Standing close to him had been the renowned Dr Cawas Lalcaca. Having spent part of the evening chatting to Sir Curzon, Dr Lalcaca had, according to Dhingra's account, attempted to intervene and was shot in the chest. Dr Lalcaca, who had been spending a year on sabbatical in London, died on the way to hospital.

The murders caused outrage. Immediately *The Globe* called it 'a political assassination', and went into a rather colourful description:

> Suddenly, in the twinkling of an eye as it were, and to the stupefaction of those around, shots rang out, and Sir Curzon fell on his back on the stairs. An Indian student was standing in front holding a smoking revolver. One bullet had shattered Sir Curzon's right eye, another bullet had pierced his face just below the other eye. Doctor Lalcaca fell with a bullet through his chest. There were other doctors among the guests and immediate medical attention was forthcoming, further assistance being summoned ... however ... Sir Curzon 's fate was sealed, and life was certified to be extinct.

A police officer, who happened to be passing the Institute, arrested Dhingra – already restrained and disarmed by other guests – who was carrying a written statement of his motives.

The *Christchurch Times* reported that that Dhingra's family had been in contact with Sir Curzon, asking him to offer the young man some advice because they feared he was 'getting into a dangerous circle'. And that Sir Curzon had written to him, but that this had only caused further resentment.

The Zoroastrian funeral of Dr Lalcaca took place at Brookwood Cemetery, also known as the London Necropolis; it was built near Woking and at one time was the largest cemetery in the world. Among the floral tributes was one from Lady Wyllie inscribed: 'These flowers are sent by the wife of Sir Curzon Wyllie, in ever grateful remembrance of the brave and noble man who lost his life on the night of 1 July in trying to save her beloved husband and others, with deepest sympathy.'

The Old Bailey trial took place before the end of the month. When asked to plead, Dhingra said, 'Whatever I did was an act of patriotism and justice which was justified. The only thing I have to say is in the statement which I believe you have got.' The judge, however, ruled that the written statement could not be read out in court and a plea of 'not guilty' was entered. Dhingra was found guilty on both counts and sentenced to death. He was hanged at Pentonville prison on 17 August 1909.

Three days later the *Bicester Herald* was one of the newspapers that printed his statement:

> I admit the other day I attempted to shed English blood as a humble revenger for the inhuman hangings and deportations of patriotic youths. In this attempt I have consulted none but my own conscience. I have conspired with none but my own duty ... I believe that a nation held down by foreign bayonet is in a perpetual state of war, since open battle is rendered impossible to a disarmed race. I attacked by surprise; since guns were denied me, I drew forth my pistol and fired ... The only lesson required in India at present is to learn how to die, and the only way to teach it is by dying ourselves. Therefore, I died, and glory in my martyrdom.

It was, perhaps, remarkable that so few such events had happened on British shores, and the population here saw the Empire as a force for good, a reflection of a strong nation and a place of opportunity. But a successful empire needed the migration of its people to its far-flung territories. It needed governors and managers, entrepreneurs, and farmers to control, expand its influence and reap the rewards.

The nineteenth century had been a boom era for migration away from Britain, often because of a wish to leave troubles, lack of opportunity, and poverty behind. Most emigres had travelled to the United States, but there had been a steady stream of migrants to British territories overseas. Very many of them had returned home to Britain, because their fortune had been made, or lost, or because settling down in a strange place, with an often radically different climate, did not always prove easy.

At the beginning of the twentieth century, migration continued – between 1901 and 1910, 2.3 million people left Britain for new lives abroad – but now the vast majority chose the Empire. Often, they had relatives or friends who had already made the journey and who had been able to regale them with tales of their successful new lives and the beauty of their surroundings. Or at least guarantee them a secure job. Emigrees of the early twentieth century were simply better informed at what to expect – and they were migrating towards, rather than away from, somewhere.

The pages of newspapers regularly featured advertisements relating to migration. Like the *Peterhead Sentinel and Buchan Journal* of 19 March 1904, where the Allan Line and State Line advertised 'well-appointed steamers sail regularly from Glasgow to New York, Boston, Philadelphia, Quebec, Montreal, Halifax Nova Scotia and St John's Newfoundland, carrying goods and passengers at lowest rates to all leading points'.

Alexander Robertson's travel agency sold tickets from a number of different shipping companies like Anchor Line, which sailed to all parts of America from Glasgow and Liverpool, and to the Mediterranean, Egypt and India, to where they had operated new steamers of 6,000 tons which left Glasgow and Liverpool for Bombay and Calcutta at 'short intervals ... Splendid Passenger Accommodation Very Moderate Fares'.

The same page had advertisements from United Lines – sailing to Canada from Liverpool and to Alexandria in Egypt; Dominion – from Liverpool to Quebec and Montreal as well as Gibraltar and Egypt. White Star Line's Royal Mail twin-screw steamships ran monthly from Liverpool to Albany, Adelaide, Melbourne, Sydney and New Zealand. Orient offered the same service, and Union Castle line ran steamers 'to all ports of Cape colony'. The New Zealand shipping company had a Royal Mail line of steamers bound for Tasmania, Melbourne and Sydney, while Canadian Pacific Railway sailed from London, Liverpool and Southampton to America, Australia, New Zealand, China and Japan. The Shaw-Saville and Albion Company took passengers to all ports in New Zealand. The Glasgow Shipping Company's Clyde line of Clipper packets to Melbourne and the Imperial direct West Indian mail service between Avonmouth in Bristol and Jamaica rounded off the list.

In 1906, James Burt's Bookseller, Stationer and Emigration Agent of Kirkaldy used the pages of the *Leven Advertiser & Wemyss Gazette* to declare itself 'The place to book your passage for Canada, United States, S. Africa, Australia, New Zealand and all part of the World.' Under a rather romantic image of a sailing vessel, it warned potential emigrees to 'book early ... boats filling rapidly'. For those wishing to make their new lives in New Zealand, New South Wales and Western Australia, there were reduced passages. For 'approved agriculturalists and domestic servants' bound for Queensland, there was the offer of 'free passages'. As an enticement to settlers to Rhodesia, the promise of 'specially low rates' and 'cards of introductions', and assistance in finding employment was given.

The following year there was still great encouragement to move to Australia, with the Dominion holding its own stand at the Highland Agricultural Show. The Canadian Government, through Thomas Cook & Co, promoted its own 'Organised Emigration' where 'farmhands, railwaymen and domestic servants etc' would be given 'all the benefits ... free of charge'.

In October 1909, the pages of the *Guernsey Evening Press* brought news from the Emigrants' Information Office in London that demand for general migrants seemed to have fallen away. Canada, with the cold months ahead, had no more demand for 'all classes of emigrants, except for female domestic servants' until the next spring, warning that no one should travel there unless they were invited by friends, or in possession of a work contract that would last though winter. They also reminded would-be incomers that they must arrive with $25 (£5 4s) and an onward ticket to their chosen final destination. Those sent to Canada by 'British charitable societies, or by public funds', must have the correct papers approving them as 'suitable settlers for Canada'. Should any of them find that, within two years, they had 'become a public charge, or an inmate of a penitentiary, gaol, prison or hospital, or charitable institution', they might well be sent back to the United Kingdom along with their dependants.

Australia, meanwhile, still had plenty of opportunities. Those arriving in Queensland and Western Australia 'may obtain free grants of 160 acres of land on easy conditions of residence and improvement'.

Mechanics were not nearly so in demand as 'thoroughly competent carpenters, bricklayers, blacksmiths and other skilled men', although they were still warned not to travel unless they had sufficient money to see them through until they found a job.

New Zealand wanted only 'farmers with capital, bona-fide farm labourers, and female domestic servants'. The South African colonies now had very little requirement for migrant workers, save for a few female domestic servants. Young women wishing to apply were required first to contact the South African Colonisation Society.

The British government remained keen to encourage British families to migrate across the Empire. It was also keen to continue propagating interest in, and knowledge of, what it would call 'Greater Britain Overseas'. To this end, in 1911 a huge Festival of Empire was held at the Crystal Palace. Initially planned for the previous year, but postponed due to Edward VII's death, it was re-scheduled to coincide with coronation celebrations for George V.

Described in its own literature as 'a social gathering of the British family', the Festival was intended to assure the 'firmer welding of those invisible bonds which hold together the greatest empire the world has ever known'. It was a celebration of all things British and Empire, a showcase for its resources, products and culture. It was not the first pro-Imperial propaganda exercise of the Edwardian era – the 1905 Colonial and Indian Exhibition at Crystal Palace and the 1909 Imperial International Exhibition at London's White City had been impressive, but this was on a far grander scale. The Crystal Palace had been designed by Joseph Paxton for the Great Exhibition on Hyde Park sixty years earlier. It had subsequently been reconstructed to an amended design in parkland on Penge Peak next to Sydenham Hill.

The Festival stretched for 250 acres. Ten miles of roads and paths were laid, and millions of plants, trees and bushes were put in the ground. Under the watchful direction of theatre designer Leolyn G. Hart, some 300 buildings were constructed – all the work of 7,000 workers, of which 100 were painters.

Britain's most impressive colonial possessions were there for all to see – at least in miniature. Australia, New Zealand, Canada and South Africa were all represented by two-thirds replicas of their government buildings alongside 'typical' scenes of their lands. For New Zealand, geysers and a 'wood-exporting port'. For Canada, orchards. Australia had its vineyards and a 'woodman's cottage'; India had architecture, tea gardens, a historical and art exhibition, and 'a jungle'. South Africa showed its gold and diamond mines. There were also a Malay village, several Irish cottages, a sugar plantation representing the Crown Colonies, a colonial tobacco plantation, a 'Cingalese town', and at least one building described as a 'native hut'. Attempts were made, using the latest technology, to provide a realistic simulation of the varied landscapes around the Empire by mass re-landscaping and the use of vast painted canvases.

Visitors boarded a small-gauge railway, with open-sided cars named the 'All-Red Route' after the telegraph network that linked the Empire. It made a circular tour of the various scenes. Local fauna was represented by a mixture of stuffed wild animals and living ones, like the fish brought over from Newfoundland and the 1,000 wild rabbits from Australia. Publicity declared it 'the most wonderful trip ever afforded to the public' with a unique chance to see 'colonials and natives at work'. Among them were African tribesmen, Māori villagers and Malay people who were constructing houses. In many cases, visitors were seeing actual people from the lands depicted; in others they saw only mannequins. One souvenir picture postcard gave visitors some idea of what it termed the 'Native Types' they might see, and which included 'Punjab', 'Bombay', 'Jeypore', 'Madras', 'Zulu' and 'South American Carribees'. Twice a day, at the Football Ground, visitors were entertained with 'Wild Australia' consisting of several elements: 'Life in the Bush, Exhibition of Whip-Cracking, Riding Bucking Horses, Kangaroo Shoots, Boomerang Throwing etc. Admission from 6d. Boxes 3/6'.

'Bostock's Zoological Congress and New Arenic Exhibition of Trained Wild Animals of the Empire' was promised to be 'The most striking and instructive animal Exhibition ever shown to the British Public – A show that no one should miss.' Each Saturday evening there was a Grand Military Tattoo on the Pageant Grounds – a 'Magnificent Stirring Spectacle – 500 torchbearers, Nine Guards' Bands, under the direction of Lt Dr J. MacKenzie Rogan MVO. Preceded by a realistic military display.' The 'Mighty Mountain Railway and Water-shoot – 'no scenic railway has ever attained the thrilling sensations of this. Lightning dashes through the valleys, over the mountains, across the chasms, ending up with the wild excitement of the water-shoot.' There was a depiction of the Great Fire of London on 1666 – 'a triumph of scenic art and wondrous realism', as well as further amusement rides and activities, fine art exhibitions, band concerts, and a 'Fair of Fashions'. Part of the park was devoted to British home life and included a 'Mediaeval Maze', the 'Small Holdings and Country Life section' and a 'Tudor village'.

The Festival of Empire opened on 12 May 1911 and closed on 1 October. On the first day there was a 'Grand Opening Concert', attended by the royal family, and featuring an Imperial Choir of 4,500, with music provided by the Queen's Hall Orchestra, the London Symphony Orchestra and a special Festival of Empire Military Band performing various patriotic works by Elgar. Entrance to the Festival site cost one shilling – the equivalent of perhaps three or four cinema tickets – although several of the performances and elements charged an additional fee for entry. Nevertheless, publicity for the Festival declared:

> Never was one shilling endowed with such magic power. It admits you to the charms, the wealth, the wonders of the Empire that girdles the globe. 1,000 times more vivid when you see it than when you read about it – a site that never was possible before – an opportunity for interest and amusement that may never offer itself again in your lifetime.

An important element of the Festival was the highly impressive outdoor Pageant of London, which was a huge undertaking, according to the official guidebook designed to show 'the gradual growth and development of the English nation, as seen in the history of this, the Empire City'. It sought to anchor London as both the physical and sentimental centre of the Empire. Consisting of thirty-two separate scenes and divided into four parts – each of which was a separate show, one or two of which were performed each day. The entire pageant was shown in its entirety twice a week between Mondays, Wednesdays, Thursdays and Saturdays. In order to see the entire story, a visitor would have to attend on at least three days. It was sited in its own vast 'Pageant Grounds' at one edge of the park, on a site later used for the Crystal Palace Bowl. The Pageant ran during the summer months between June and mid-September, premiering on 8 June in front of the Duke of Connaught and, it was reported, a huge crowd, some 70,000 of them from Camberwell.

Packed audiences continued to attend, 10,000 could be seated in the amphitheatre-style grandstand alone. Across the run, more than one million visitors, paying between 1s and 21s, watched the pageant. At the time it was reported to have cost the organisers £66,000 (more than £9 million at 2024's value).

The Pageant was truly spectacular. The *Croydon Express* of 10 June declared that it was 'on a scale never approached in magnitude since pageantry became a popular form of entertainment'. The creation of Frank Lascelles, the so-called 'Pageant Master'. The music, much of it contemporary, was provided by twenty composers that included Ralph Vaughan Williams and Gustav Holst. Sir Hubert Parry was on the Pageant Music Advisory Committee. The talents of some of the very best experts in the land were utilised to create the Pageant. Sir Aston Webb, RA, the man who had designed the Victoria and Albert Museum and would go on to design the new façade of Buckingham Palace in 1913, was responsible for the design of the grandstand.

Lascelles was, effectively, dramatising the history of London to celebrate 'the magnificence, glory and honour of the Empire and the Mother Country'. The Pageant featured what was claimed were the largest tapestry and carpet in the world, and was on a vast scale. The first scene of Part One was entitled 'Primitive London. The Dawn of British History', and was set at the junction of the Fleet and Thames rivers. With a hill-top fortress far in the background, and a Druid temple at in the foreground, the Celtic inhabitants learned of an imminent invasion. Battle-weary troops returned; Druids made a sacrifice to gain favour with the tribe's deity. The scene ended with the arrival of the Roman army, Julius Caesar at its head, ultimately defeating the Celts and seizing London. As the next scene opened, a Roman wall had been erected and the Druid temple replaced by a Roman one dedicated to the goddess Diana. And so the Pageant went on … through the times of King Alfred and Aethelred the Unready, and battles against the Vikings. Then the Norman Conquest and the Plantagenets. The first part ended with a recreation of a tournament at Smithfield, complete with fighting and horses.

Part Two began with Chaucer's fictional Canterbury Pilgrims, as they gathered at the Tabard Inn in Southwark. This was followed by the factual Wat Tyler and the Peasants' Revolt; and the great celebrations marking Henry V's victory at Agincourt and the defeat of Richard III at Bosworth. The Tudor period was depicted by a May Day celebration in 'Merrie England', complete with maypole dancing, an archery contest, Morris dancers; even Robin Hood and His Merry Men made a surprise appearance in the capital. Elizabeth I was depicted knighting Francis Drake and rallying the troops at Tilbury.

Part Three moved quickly, beginning with the inevitable depiction of Empire with ships of the East India Company docking in and trading from London, and the departure of the *Mayflower* from Plymouth. James I was shown meeting with Pocahontas, before the Civil War, the Commonwealth period, and the Restoration of the Monarchy. The Plague and the Great Fire followed, with celebrations as London is rebuilt and life returns to normal. The Empire theme continued with Captain Cook setting sail. Part Three closes with what the programme calls 'The Great War' – the wars against Napoleonic France, and a touching depiction of Nelson's body being brought home by Hardy, followed by a celebration of Britain's continuing relationships with its allies in the war – the Prince of Orange, the King of Prussia, and the Emperor of Russia.

Part Four focused on the expansion of the Empire and showed various encounters between the British and native populations, ending with – the occasional show of force and some strife aside – happy cooperation and celebration between the two cultures. The scenes covering India were particularly decadent, complete with 'elephants' and 'camels'.

The final scene was described as 'The Masque Imperial – an Allegory of the Advantages of Empire', and reveals much about the general attitude towards the Empire, or at least the one the government rather wished its citizens would buy into. A great new power, named 'Britannia', faces a trial to prove her worth to the 'World's Dominion'. Much was made of the seven 'Queens of the World's Destiny' and the 'Damozels of Death', and of hope triumphing under Britannia's watch. A colourful finale showed the heralds of the home nations followed by representatives from across the Empire.

A smaller part of the Festival was the 'Inter-Empire Championships', for which teams from Australasia, Canada, South Africa and the United Kingdom competed in four sports – athletics, swimming, heavyweight boxing and middleweight wrestling. The trophy, a 2ft 6in silver cup donated by Lord Lonsdale, was won by Canada. It was proclaimed in advertisements to be 'The First Meeting of its Kind Ever Held'. But it would not be the last; the event is considered to be the forerunner of the Empire – and since 1970, Commonwealth – Games. Throughout the summer a number of other sporting competitions took place as part of the Festival under the banner of 'Great Imperial Sports Meetings', and promised 'interesting sports meeting twice weekly June to October'. And so it proved. At the West London Cycling Association Sports Meeting on 2 June, motorcyclist Harry Martin – already holder of the 200-mile world record, broke the 5-mile record by a remarkable 21.45 seconds. Three days later saw the Highgate Harriers' Monster Athletic Meeting. Two days after that, the Kite and Model Aeroplanes Association held their event. On 10 June, the St Martin's Harriers, a GPO team, held an athletics and cycling competition on the Sports Ground; at the Lower Lake, the Amateur Swimming Club held a swimming and polo competition; and, at the Football Ground, the Base Ball Association held a game between teams representing Crystal Palace and West Ham.

The important aim of encouraging emigration of British families across the Empire was not forgotten. In support of the showcases that each area had within the Festival, the daily printed programme – sold ostensibly to provide important visitor information – carried advertisements to this end. The High Commissioner for New Zealand promoted its 'splendid pastoral country', and promised farmers, farmhands, and single female domestic servants reduced fares. British

Columbia in Canada was promoted as 'eminently suitable for those seeking a home beyond the seas', with the added benefits of a better standard of living and lower taxes.

In Africa, at the turn of the twentieth century, British influence extended from the west, across to the north-east, thanks to Britain's control over the Suez Canal from 1882, and towards the very southern tip of the continent. British colonies now covered much of Africa from modern Nigeria, Sierra Leone, Ghana, Gambia, Egypt, Sudan, Kenya, Uganda, Tanzania, Malawi, Zambia, Zimbabwe, Botswana and South Africa. And it was in the southern part of Africa that Britain found one of its greatest challenges that would lead to a brutal, and domestically unpopular war that would blight the first seventeen months of Edward VII's reign.

CHAPTER 3

A BACKGROUND OF SLAUGHTER

> The modern Boer. The most formidable antagonist who ever cross the path of Imperial Britain
>
> Sir Arthur Conan Doyle

On Monday, 2 June 1902, thousands of people dodged tramcars as they weaved their way through the streets of Newcastle upon Tyne. The local gas board illuminated its premises, medical students in their caps and gowns paraded at the Central railway station, singing *Dolly Grey* and other popular songs, and a Salvation Army band played *God Save The King*.

The *Newcastle Evening Chronicle* reported that the festivities went on long after midnight as people:

> jubilated in celebration of the conclusion of the long, drawn-out hostilities in South Africa. Although there was horseplay now and again, and rough behaviour occasionally, there was nothing to seriously call for the interference of the police authorities, who, under the exceptional circumstances, allowed a little more latitude to roistering youngsters than is usually permitted.

As in every city, town and village in what was now Edwardian Britain, the people of Tyneside were heralding the end of the Boer War, a conflict that had cast a long shadow over the first months of the Edwardian era.

European settlers had been colonising west and southern Africa since the fifteenth century. They established small ports for trade and transportation on the route between what we know as Asia and the Americas. First to arrive had been the Portuguese followed by the Dutch. Around the southern Cape, farmers – known as Boers, from the Dutch word for farmer – worked the land for several generations. They were Afrikaans speakers, of Dutch, German and French Huguenot origin. They were followed by the British – in the form of the English who had established a presence in West Africa during Tudor times – then the French and other northern Europeans.

In the late eighteenth century Britain expanded her interests to the south and took control of the Cape. This led to a mass migration, known as the Great Trek, of Boers who had formed their own sub-culture and wished to escape British rule by moving to the interior of what is now South Africa. There they established what became the Boer colonies of Orange Free State (roughly the land now known as Free State) and Transvaal (now divided into Gauteng, Limpopo and Mpumalanga). Subsequent discoveries of valuable minerals such as diamonds led not only to the industrialisation of previously agricultural communities, but also brought the Boers and Britain into dispute.

Skirmishes over territorial control had led to the conflict, often called the 'First Boer War', of 1880–1 between Britain and Transvaal. It had lasted for only ten weeks, and ended with Britain restoring Transvaal as technically independent, but subject to British approval.

Remarkably, given that neither side was entirely content, the fragile truce and a superficially peaceful coexistence held for eighteen years, until the discovery of gold deposits in the Boer territories. That sparked a great influx of people, many of them British, seeking to exploit the mineral. The Boers maintained control by denying foreigners, or 'Uitlanders', any political power. Without any political clout within the Boer territories it was unlikely that British mining companies would be favoured.

Hoping to put pressure on the Boers, Britain brought in military reinforcements. On 9 October 1899 the Boers demanded that Britain remove not only those reinforcements but also all troops from the shared border. Britain stood firm. Two days later, the Boer republics of the Orange Free State and Transvaal declared war on Britain.

In Britain, politicians, military commanders and the majority of the public alike were confident that it could prevail with ease. It quickly became clear, however, that this was not the case. In the early days of the conflict, the Boers outnumbered the British, and their use of unorthodox military tactics confounded the more formally organised British troops. As farmers who relied upon their guns for security and food, the Boers were expert marksmen, equipped with modern weapons and artillery. By the turn of the year, they had taken Natal and the Cape, and the towns of Ladysmith, Kimberley and Mafeking were besieged. All of which came as a great shock to Britons unused to reading about military setbacks.

While the war was widely supported, with hundreds of thousands of young men volunteering to fight for what was then still 'Queen and country', there was also considerable opposition from the outset. This took many forms. Quakers, women's groups, Liberals, socialists, suffragists, trades unionists and even Irish nationalists all took a vehement anti-war stance. For the most part, these groups were either pacifist, or anti-colonial. There were suspicions that the war was being driven by those keen to get their hands of South Africa's gold and diamonds. Liberal MP David Lloyd George also suggested that the Secretary of State for the Colonies, Joseph Chamberlain, and members of his family, had shares in munitions firms that were making great profits out of the conflict. And then there were those otherwise ardent supporters of Empire, and certainly not pacifists, who simply found it distasteful for one Protestant nation to fight against another over African lands. Criticism from abroad also hampered British confidence in the morality of the war.

Within the Liberal Party both the South African Conciliation Committee and the Stop the War Committee worked to coalesce dissenting voices. With most major newspapers – the notable exceptions being the *Manchester Guardian* and *Westminster Gazette* – broadly in support of the war, anti-war groups had to rely on the distribution of their own leaflets to convey their views to a wider public.

Once mass reinforcements arrived in Africa, the war began to turn in Britain's favour. The besieged British cities of Kimberley and

Ladysmith were relieved in February 1900, followed by Mafeking in May. Britain then took control of Johannesburg and Pretoria and, by October, Orange Free State and Transvaal had also succumbed. Joseph Chamberlain asserted that the war was all but 'over'. In response to the apparent successes, the so-called 'Khaki election' of 1900, saw the ruling Conservative government of Lord Salisbury returned in a landslide victory.

But the Boers' guerrilla tactics of stalking and ambushing continued to prove effective against the British. An increasingly frustrated General Horatio Herbert Kitchener, in command of British forces, looked to new methods to assert the upper hand. He decided to deny the Boers their supplies and the security of their homes. He ordered advancing British troops to ensure the mass removal of tens of thousands of Boers, many of them women and children, from their towns, villages, and farms to new segregated 'concentration camps'.

Farmhouses, agricultural buildings and even crops were destroyed, and when news of those tactics began to drift on to the pages of British newspapers, there was little handwringing from either editors or their readers. What did begin to cut through to the public conscience, however, was the worrying humanitarian situation emerging in the military-controlled concentration camps, in particular those holding women and children.

Much of what we know about the camps came through the testimony of Emily Hobhouse, the secretary of the South African Conciliation Committee. In December 1900 she had learned about a camp at Port Elizabeth where conditions were unhygienic and where there were shortages of vital supplies. By the time the new king came to the throne the following month, she had sailed for South Africa to supervise the distribution of aid. She would soon learn that there were more than forty other Boer camps and that conditions in several were far worse than she had anticipated. Through a family connection with the British High Commissioner, Alfred Milner, and with the approval of Kitchener, she managed to secure the use of two railway trucks which allowed her to transport twelve tons of supplies.

Hobhouse compiled her own 'Report of a Visit to the Camps of Women and Children in the Cape and Orange River Colonies', which she would present to the British government in June 1901. It testified to truly appalling conditions in some camps where up to three family groups occupied a single tent, soap was in short supply and fuel was so limited that there was reluctance to use any to make river water safe by boiling.

She wrote: 'I call this camp system a wholesale cruelty ... To keep these camps going is murder to the children.'

While being scathing of the military, Hobhouse admitted, 'I can't help melting a little when they are very humble and confess that the whole thing is a grievous and gigantic blunder and presents an almost insoluble problem, and they don't know how to face it.'

The military authorities might have been doing their best, but with 'entire villages rooted up and dumped in a strange, bare place', the situation was dire.

> I was at the camp to-day, and just in one little corner this is the sort of thing I found – The nurse, underfed and overworked, just sinking on to her bed, hardly able to hold herself up, after coping with some thirty typhoid and other patients, with only the untrained help of two Boer girls, cooking as well as nursing to do herself. Next tent, a six-months' baby gasping its life out on its mother's knee. Two or three others drooping sick in that tent. Next, a girl of 21 lay dying on a stretcher. The father, a big, gentle Boer, kneeling beside her; while, next tent, his wife was watching a child of 6 also dying, and one of about 5 drooping. Already this couple had lost three children in the hospital and so would not let these go, though I begged hard to take them out of the hot tent. I can't describe what it is to see these children lying about in a state of collapse. It's just exactly like faded flowers thrown away. And one has to stand and look on at such misery, and be able to do almost nothing.

Disease was common in the camps. At Bloemfontein, measles and typhoid – apparently common in the town – had become rampant in the camps. Food was in short supply – certainly not sufficient to maintain robust immune systems. The situation worsened when Dr Norman Pern, the medic in charge, rejected meat brought to the camp because he learned that some of the cattle had been unhealthy before slaughter. That earned him a stiff rebuke from Captain Arthur Hume – the superintendent of the camp – a man of whom Hobhouse had been particularly critical.

For his part, Hume appeared to have good intentions:

> It is my object to make the people under my charge, forget as much as possible that they are here under compulsion, and as far as is compatible with sanitary and health conditions I leave them to themselves ... Further, I think that the treatment meted out to those in refugee camps will have a material influence for good or evil in the future settlement of the country. I am therefore very careful in my dealings with them.

Outbreaks of disease were also common at military posts. Sir Arthur Conan Doyle, the creator of Sherlock Holmes, served as a volunteer doctor at the Langman Field Hospital at Bloemfontein in the spring of 1900. He would later testify that more than 14,000 British soldiers had died from disease, a far greater number than the 8,000 who had been killed in combat. And that at his over-burdened military hospital fifty to sixty soldiers had died each day.

When Hobhouse returned to Britain she was determined to tell her story. She gave twenty-eight, largely well-received, talks, many of them to Quaker groups and other religious gatherings at places that included Friends' Meeting Houses in Bath and Leeds, the Temperance Institute in Southport, the Master's Lodge of Balliol College, Oxford, and halls in Portsmouth, Bradford, Bristol, Liverpool and Hull.

Hobhouse's testimony eventually led to the establishment of a formal commission. Its team of official investigators was led by women's rights activist Millicent Fawcett and generally corroborated what Hobhouse had found.

The military denied rumours that British soldiers had taken Boer families from their homes by force at a moment's notice. And also that families had been forced on to cattle trucks, stating that the trucks were the very same ones which had been used in the rescue of British refugees, and on which the military themselves regularly travelled. That the families had not had all their possessions taken away, but had been told to identify their most important possessions to bring with them. Anything left behind, and deemed useful to the enemy's war effort, was destroyed. Some claimed that the Boers had not been permitted to take food on the journey. This, too, was denied and the point was made that, if this had been the case, the soldiers would have had to share their own rations with the civilians.

In Britain, these stories were causing growing concern. In October 1901 *The Morning Leader* reported on a meeting of the National Sunday School Convention, held in Birmingham, at which a resolution was carried requesting the government take urgent steps to 'diminish the awful death rate of children in some of the concentration camps'.

Some elements, however, were not all that sympathetic to the plight of their fellow humans – as outspoken Liverpool-based Baptist minister Charles Aked was to discover. He declared:

> Great Britain cannot win the battles without resorting to the last despicable cowardice of the most loathsome cur on earth – the act of striking a brave man's heart through his wife's honour and his child's life. The cowardly war has been conducted by methods of barbarism … the concentration camps have been murder camps.

Disgruntled members of the crowd followed him home and broke the windows of his house.

Others did speak out. In June 1901, John Morley, MP, long a vocal opponent of the war, gave a speech at Montrose. He called out those who validated the war on the grounds that the Boers had no right to African lands, having taken it from native Africans, and ignored Britain's role on the continent which amounted to the very same thing. Protests were held, meetings arranged in places like Canning Town and Northampton, letters written and declarations issued.

Until eventually, in October 1901, control of the camps was taken from the military and handed to the civil authorities, and newspapers across Britain, like the *Ashbourne News*, acknowledged that under the new regime conditions were better, and although those now running the camps were 'desperately overworked', they were making immediate improvements to carry out the recommendations of Fawcett's 'Ladies' Commission'. Extra doctors, nurses and other officials were being called in. Yet the death rates remained concerning. According to the newspaper, in September in one area alone of 35,528 adult 'inmates', 245 had died, while 1,124 of 29,786 children also perished. By the end of the war, in just eighteen months of their operation, the concentration camps had seen the deaths of some 26,370 Boers. An astonishing 24,000 of those had been infants and children under 16. It was a statistic that would taint Britain's reputation internationally.

Many military lives were also lost. By February 1901, the first few weeks of Edward VII's reign, the war had been raging for sixteen months. General Kitchener offered the Boers what the British considered generous peace terms. In return for becoming crown colonies under British rule, the Boer republics would eventually have self-government within the Empire. All 'coloured persons' would be granted the same, rather limited, legal rights they had enjoyed in the British Cape Colony, with a guarantee that should they ever be given the vote it would be 'so limited as to secure the just predominance of the white race'.

As determined a fight as the Boers had put up, they were inevitably beaten by a larger, stronger force. An agreement, however, was not reached until 31 May 1902. Under the Treaty of Vereeniging, the Boers accepted British sovereignty in return for several concessions, including the use of both English and Afrikaans in schools and law courts, eventual self-government, and £3 million compensation for the destruction of Boer farms and property.

The Treaty had not been signed until late in the evening and word did not reached Britain until the following day. When news of peace did arrive, in most places at just after 6pm, it was greeted with a heady, yet measured, mixture of joy and relief. The pages of the *Derby Evening Telegraph* reported various scenes across the nation and noted that, within minutes of the news, the streets, electric tramways, trains and ferries of Liverpool were 'taxed to their utmost in pouring the excited and thankful people into the city'.

From its own patch the Derby paper reported that the news had been slower to spread:

> At the great majority of the local places of worship there was absolutely no reference to the momentous intelligence, and the congregations dispersed without anyone being aware of what had happened. There were, however, one or two exceptions to this rule. Just before the conclusion of the service at St Alkmund's a note was passed to the vicar and the news was announced by him from the pulpit. The congregation afterwards joined heartily in singing a hymn of thanksgiving.

A short service of prayer was held at the town's Victoria Street Congregational Church. Nearby, at St Werburgh's, the good news was announced much to the surprise of congregants. And, before long, the Sunday evening promenaders were sharing rumours of a peace that they scarcely dared to believe: 'It was some time before [they could] realise that they bore the hallmark of authority', the crowd being 'rather inclined to attribute it to one of those freaks of rumour.'

It was only when the newspaper offices put out placards proclaiming the news that 'universal expressions of thankfulness broke out across the town'. 'Flags were held up, although there was no ringing of bells, very little cheering and no singing. The people obviously delighted at the news, but they received it all the same with a sober restraint that was probably the best test of their sincerity and depth of feeling.'

The following morning, as was the case in cities, towns and villages across the nation,

> the news was announced by a merry peal on the bells ... there was also a liberal supply of bunting, not only in the principal streets but also from the humble houses in the

less frequented thoroughfares ... the flag floated from more than one house that has a representative at the front, and the emotions with which it was hoisted were as may be imagined not merely national, but personal.

The following morning the nation's newspapers made much of the news, several quoting the words of *The Standard* which had proclaimed both its 'heartfelt gratitude towards the brave men' that had brought about victory, and a grudging admiration for the 'most valiant adversaries whom it has ever fallen to the lot of the British and colonial troops to encounter'.

It might almost have sounded like the summary of a hard-fought international football match, such was the jolly spin on events. Indeed, a week later the *Guernsey Evening Press* was quoting a correspondent who asserted: 'It is now shown that the concentration camps have proved a blessing in disguise to the Boers. The inmates are happy and healthy, and are being taught trades.'

In truth, the Second Boer War had been utterly wretched. In total it is estimated that close to 100,000 lives had been lost, including at least 14,000 Boer and 20,000 British troops. The total of non-combatant deaths was far higher, both inside and outside the camps. Although the war had ostensibly been between two white opponents, there had been many deaths among the Black population. The staggering statistics, hidden for many decades, reveal that there were more than sixty camps for Black 'refugees', perhaps as many as eighty-nine, many of them operated as labour camps. Deaths from malnutrition, disease or work accidents among Black people held in camps were reputedly extremely high, although not officially recorded, and are estimated to range from 13,000 to 20,000.

The terrible irony of the Second Boer War was that the majority of inhabitants, those who had ancestral and moral rights to the land and had suffered so much during a conflict inflicted upon them, were all but left out of peace. Under the Treaty of Vereeniging the thorny question of whether Black Africans would be permitted to vote was pushed forward indefinitely to the day when self-governance began. It was already clear that Black Africans living in the Boer areas would not be permitted to vote. Many of the Black population had fought alongside the British, or been innocent spectators, but they would gain little from the peace. Instead, they would have many decades of suffering to come under a system of apartheid informally operated by the Afrikaners, and officially sanctioned into South African law in 1948.

Even in Imperial Britain, however, there were people willing to speak up for native Black Africans. In 1913, Emily Hobhouse wrote a speech for the unveiling of a memorial to the war. In it she pleaded for all those who had died in the camps to be remembered, regardless of the colour of their skin: 'Does not justice bid to remember today how many thousands of the dark race perished also in the concentration camps in a quarrel that was not theirs?'

At the war's end the foreign press had focused on the role of King Edward VII. From Paris the Central News Agency reported that in an article entitled 'The King's Peace', the newspaper *Le Gaulois* 'rejoices at the cessation of the conflict'. *Le Gaulois* said, 'The King is a resolute partisan of the old English traditions, like his mother, and the prolongation of the war was contrary to those traditions.' *La République* commented, 'The conclusion of peace is to be attributed to the influence of King Edward VII [who] has therefore earned not only the gratitude of his country and the praise of the civilised world, but he has raised the royal prestige and has acquired an immense and deserved popularity.'

'The King', said *Le Gaulois*, 'wished for peace. His heart grieved that the Coronation should have for a background slaughter and the horrors of war.'

CHAPTER 4

VIVAT REX!

It was a sight indeed. They had white satin dresses and long trains of crimson velvet and ermine capes – trains and their coronets in hands. They came by twos or threes and dozens and were marvellous to behold. I never saw so many jewels in my life.

Edwin Austin Abbey,
official Coronation artist.

Late June 1902: Britain's streets are swathed in red, white and blue, hung with flags and bunting, decorated with garlands and greenery. The nation is preparing for its first coronation in more than six decades.

Almost eighteen months had passed since the death of Queen Victoria. Now the days leading up to the scheduled crowning of her son saw theatres and public buildings bedecked with flowers. Businesses and homes displayed images of Edward VII and his queen, Alexandra. Britain was finally in the mood to celebrate again.

Edward's coronation had been set for 26 June, sixty-four years almost to the day since his mother's. For months, detailed plans had been drawn up to turn the whole country into a riot of colour and celebration. The *Derby Daily Telegraph* declared that everything in the East Midlands town was in 'apple pie order'. Derbeians prepared food for public teas and dinners, and local shops advertised their own merchandise of decorations and souvenirs as work went on to dress the town centre and every neighbourhood. It was the same in every city, town and village in the country, while across the Empire the final touches were also being made to celebratory events long in the planning.

Inevitably, nowhere was more heavily decorated than London. The *Illustrated Sporting and Dramatic News* of Tuesday, 17 June 1902 reported: 'For weeks past London has been transformed from its usual appearance into a timber town in preparation for the gorgeous ceremony of next week, the first of its kind, owing to the length of life vouchsafe to our late lamented Queen Victoria, many of us will have seen.'

There was great pride, too, at the modern society that Britain now enjoyed. Readers were reminded of the many changes that had occurred during the late queen's reign, changes which now greatly benefited the citizens of the new Edwardian Era:

> Since the last coronation was solemnised, changes many and important have taken place. When Queen Victoria was crowned, stagecoaches were used by her subjects on their travels, yet in a comparatively short period of sixty years we have trains running at marvellous speed, overhead and underground railways, motor cars and huge steam yachts, not to mention other things of which they never dreamed at the date of the last coronation. In the course of the royal procession the King will progress throughout a London differing vastly from that he remembers as a boy.

Indeed, but first his subjects were soon to learn that there might be quite a wait for that procession. With just a few days to go, 'disquieting rumours' about the King's health began to circulate. Then, through newspaper reports, the country learned that in recent weeks, Edward had indeed been ailing. The 60-year-old monarch had forgone a few pre-coronation events due to what was officially termed a 'slight chill, accompanied by symptoms of lumbago', and had been advised to rest.

Then it was reported that for several mornings he had been 'confined to a couch'. Even then, however, this was not yet portrayed by the press as something to raise concerns. Particularly as many would remember that in 1877, the then Prince of Wales had contracted typhoid, the illness that had killed his father. On that occasion the public had been given regular medical bulletins on his condition. And there were real fears for his life. But he had pulled through. This time, there seemed to be no concerns for his well-being although, on 19 June, readers of the *Burton Chronicle* were among those told, 'In anticipation of the severe strain to which the King will be subjected during Coronation festivities, his Majesty's medical advisors have recommended him to forego all public engagements during the next few days.'

A statement from the Press Association offered some reassurance: 'There is ... good reason for hoping that the indisposition is temporary.'

On 23 June, the *Exeter Gazette* reported: 'The King has greatly benefited from the rest he has enjoyed during the last few days. His Majesty proposes to return to London today.'

Royal life appeared to be continuing almost as normal:

> On Saturday the King lunched in his own apartment at Windsor Castle. During the day Queen Alexandra undertook equestrian exercise in Windsor Park attended by a groom ...
> in the afternoon the King drove out in a brougham [a light horse-drawn carriage] accompanied by one of his guests. The exercise in Windsor Park lasting an hour.

Events continued more or less as planned. The Queen, without her husband but with the Prince and Princess of Wales and other members of the royal family and their guests, attended a private religious service at Windsor. Meanwhile, foreign guests continued to arrive in London for the coronation.

However, the scarcity of official detail about what still ailed the monarch left a vacuum, which led to more rumours beginning to circulate. One claimed that the King had been receiving regular treatment 'three times a week' on a throat infection from his 'Physician-Extraordinary', the Prussian-born Sir Felix Semon, Britain's leading laryngologist. People now began to wonder whether the coronation would go ahead as planned.

In fact, Edward had been suffering from appendicitis, which had first troubled him on 14 June when he and the Queen had travelled to

Aldershot for a military review. The King had begun feeling abdominal discomfort, which worsened considerably overnight until he was in severe pain and had developed a high fever – signs of a possible infection. His personal physician, Sir Francis Laking, and another doctor, Sir Thomas Barlow, both recommended that he be immediately heavily sedated. Edward was taken back to Windsor Castle. Alexandra was left to review the 30,000 waiting soldiers while her husband was officially described as being 'indisposed'.

In 1902, surgical removal of the appendix was considered a very risky procedure and was generally avoided unless it became absolutely necessary. Edward was reluctant to undergo an operation. As well as the personal risk, he was conscious of the cost, in money and time, of all the coronation preparations. He did not want to postpone.

The financial implications of a potential postponement were beginning to be felt in several major financial and insurance institutions. Initially, the King hoped his condition might improve by itself. His advisors worked to manage his schedule to allow plenty of time for rest. However, with two days to go, he developed peritonitis and his doctors advised that he needed an immediate life-saving operation to remove an abscess. the Coronation would have to be postponed. The Duke of Norfolk – as Earl Marshall, the person responsible for organising the great events of state – was informed.

Just after lunchtime on 24 June, a statement was issued from the Earl Marshal's Office: 'I have to announce that the solemnity of the Coronation of Their Majesties King Edward VII and Queen Alexandra is postponed from the 26th instant to a date hereafter to be determined.'

Far from preparing for a celebration, Edward's subjects were now left waiting for the latest news bulletin to see whether their uncrowned monarch would survive the procedure.

The *Galway Observer* summed up the mood:

> Suddenly, and as if a thunderbolt had fallen in the midst, came the fateful news which, by aid of electric telegraph, was making a circuit of the Empire and reaching far beyond its confines ere it had permeated to the sightseers who had

> taken possession of the London streets ... an operation had
> been performed upon the King between 11 and 12 o'clock

The operation was performed by the recently knighted Sir Frederick Treves, the surgeon famed some years earlier for his association with John Merrick, the so-called 'Elephant Man'.

Later that day, newspapers across the country published the good news – the operation had been 'successfully performed' and the King was 'going on well'. And the following day, while the nation paused in its decorative finishing touches, came more encouraging news. The Prince of Wales had visited his father, found him to be 'far stronger than he expected', and that, in the words of the *Westminster Gazette*, 'His Majesty conveyed to his son the reassuring intelligence that he felt actually more comfortable than before the operation.'

A medical bulletin was issued at 6.40pm, signed by Treves, Laking and two other doctors, which stated: 'His Majesty continues to make satisfactory progress, and has been much relieved by the operation.'

A few hours later came another:

> The King's condition is as good as it can be expected after so serious an operation. His strength is maintained. There is less pain, and His Majesty has taken a little nourishment. It will be some days before it will be possible to say that the King is out of danger.

Edward had sent a message to the Lord Mayor of London that the coronation dinners should go ahead as planned. He also wished his subjects throughout the Empire to continue with their planned festivities. Thursday and Friday would be the Bank Holidays previously announced and everything that could not be sensibly postponed should go ahead. It was a great relief to local organisers of thousands of events. Preparations for the massive celebrations were so far advanced – money spent and much of the food purchased already cooked.

Some events would be held back until a new date was set. The more than 2,000 bonfires which were ready for lighting would now be either removed to safety, or protected from the elements in situ. The Naval Review at Portsmouth, and the announcement of the Coronation Honours were also postponed.

Derby's mayor, Alderman Abraham Woodiwiss, hastily called together his celebrations committee, who decided that both a fireworks display and the procession and service that had been planned to coincide with events in London should be postponed. The delivery of parcels for old people and parties for children would still go ahead to take advantage of the public holiday and the midsummer weather. The decision proved fortuitous – on the rescheduled Coronation Day it rained in Derby.

Of course, there was nothing to be done about the countless medals and mugs that had already been produced showing the original date set for the coronation, save for recounting the story to succeeding generations. The new date was Saturday, 9 August.

On the new Coronation Day eve, Edward VII issued a message:

> To my people on the eve of my Coronation, an event which I look upon as one of the most solemn and important in my life, I am anxious to express to my people at home and in the colonies, and in India, my heartfelt appreciation of the deep sympathy which they have manifested towards me during the time that my life was in such imminent danger.
>
> The postponement of the ceremony owing to my illness caused, I fear, much inconvenience and trouble to all those who intended to celebrate it, but that disappointment was borne by them with admirable patience and temper. The prayers of my people for my recovery were heard, and I now offer up my deepest gratitude to Divine Providence for having preserved my life and given me strength to fulfil the important duties which devolve upon me as Sovereign of this great Empire.
>
> Edward R and I

Suddenly there were many reasons to celebrate. The coronation was finally here, the Boer War was over, and the monarch was recovering well.

In London, while the sun did not appear, Coronation Day remained dry, allowing the many thousands who lined the route of the procession to do so in comfort. There were, however, fewer in attendance than there might have been in June. Many heads of state who had travelled from overseas had long since returned home, leaving their ambassadors to represent them. Many of those living outside the capital had intended to view proceedings but were unable to travel for a second time in a year. The new date now coincided with holiday time for many Londoners who, before the rescheduling, had booked trips to the countryside and abroad. All this combined to give the coronation a more restrained atmosphere rather than the grand international occasion anticipated before the King's illness. According to J.E.C Bodley, the official historian of the event, this coronation would be 'a domestic celebration of the British race united by the influence of the Imperial Crown'.

For those now unable to attend, there was, of course, extensive newspaper coverage. The *Eastern Daily Press* reported: 'Shortly after the break of day on Saturday the booming of cannon from Hyde Park announced to the metropolis that the long expected and deferred Coronation Day had arrived. The morning opened with the promise of fine weather, and happily that was fulfilled.'

Crowds had begun arriving at Buckingham Palace before 7am. There they waited for several hours for the departure of the King and Queen, watching as various troops arrived to take their allotted position. As each band passed the Palace, striking up the National Anthem, men removed their hats and everyone cheered. It was a colourful scene. From the *Eastern Daily Press*:

> The scarlet coats of the Cornish Regiment, who lined Buckingham Gate, the blue uniforms of the Woolwich and Sandhurst cadets stationed in front of the Palace, picturesque Indian cavalry on their warlike chargers and holding aloft their gaily bedecked lances, combined to make a magnificent spectacle.

The 'Colonials', were particularly lauded. 'The magnificent panorama of khaki, gold lace, shining breastplates, waving plumes and the bejewelled turbans and gorgeous robes of the Orientals, went on till the blaze of colour became almost bewildering.'

Every so often a carriage conveying a member of the royal family in and out of the Palace would pass by and the crowd would cheer. The aged Duke of Cambridge, like his cousin Victoria, a grandchild of George III, received a particularly hearty welcome. The Duke of Connaught and his son, Prince Arthur, arrived on horseback, while Lord Roberts, Commander-in-Chief of the Forces, 'brought still more glamour into a spectacle already rich with stately pomp and military glory'.

Now the processions could begin. The first featured members of the extended royal family. In one carriage was the Duke of Cambridge with Princess Frederica of Hanover (like the King, a great-grandchild of George III) and the King's niece, Princess Alice of Albany. Next were Princes Andrew and George of Greece, the King's sister-in-law the Duchess of Albany, and the young Princess of Battenberg. Behind that were other British and foreign princes and princesses. In the final carriage were the King and Queen's daughters, Princesses Louise, Victoria and Maud, and Lady Alexandra Duff – their eldest grandchild.

According to newspapers, 'So great were the proportions of the chief pageant that the central avenue of The Mall had to be utilised for marshalling the procession, but at last the cavalcade began to move.' It was led by the Royal Horse Guards and followed by the King's Bargemaster and twelve watermen 'in their quaint and picturesque costume'.

At 11.05am, the King and Queen began their journey to Westminster Abbey in the Gold State Coach, drawn by eight beautiful postilion-driven Hanoverian Creams – then a rare, now extinct, breed of horse that had cream coats, wavy golden manes and tails, and unusual pink Roman noses and blue eyes. Their harnesses were made of red leather and gold ormolu and finished off with purple ribbons. Beside the carriage were 'gorgeous walking men' dressed in the gold-braided red and white uniform of the Royal Household while the Horse Guards provided an escort.

The most fortunate spectators lining the route took their places in giant temporary stands that had been erected for the occasion, while others – mostly servants of the royal family, with their friends – were permitted to witness the spectacle from the roof of Buckingham Palace itself.

The huge glass windows of the coach allowed onlookers a wonderful view of a reassuringly hearty-looking King and his Queen who, from time to time, bowed their heads towards their subjects. A gun salute sounded on Green Park, alerting the troops who had been resting under the shade of trees that it was time to remount their horses. Bands struck up and the chatter of the people grew steadily, reaching a crescendo as the royal couple travelled along The Mall before turning first into Horse Guards' Parade, then Whitehall where, according to the *Eastern Daily Press*, the reception was 'as unprecedented in its heartiness as was the spectacle unique in its character'.

It went on:

> Dusky warriors from the Indian Empire, clad in their brilliant and picturesque uniforms, guarded the route in conjunction with men of colour from our African and other possessions – Colonials in khaki, British cavalry in glistening helmets and breastplates, and red-coated infantry of the line. The effect was dazzling in its gorgeousness. Behind the troops were tens of thousands of Their Majesty's loyal subjects, while behind them again were tiers reaching to an almost giddy height, occupied mainly by ladies in the smartest and daintiest of summer costume.

Adding to the colourful scene, and particularly popular with the crowds, were the 'Beefeaters from the Tower', while 'Highlanders with the bagpipes and other military bands played at frequent intervals'.

The entire route was richly decorated. Outside the Houses of Parliament tall, scarlet-covered poles with gilt spear tops were linked by strings of small flags and streamers that stretched along the route.

At 11.25am, the King and Queen reached the Abbey, a few minutes behind schedule. But no one seemed to mind and the crowd cheered as the couple entered. There were some 8,000 guests, and newspapers drew particular attention to the Prime Ministers of the British Dominions, the Litunga of Barotseland (a part of Southern Africa), the Sultan of Perak (part of modern-day Malaysia) and 'thirty-one rulers of the Indian princely states', and, of course, the British Royal Family and nobility.

As the ceremony began, the King and Queen walked up the aisle to the traditional words taken from verses of Psalm 122 beginning 'I Was Glad'. The words had been part of the service since the coronation of Charles I in 1626, but this time they were sung to a splendid new tune – arranged and composed for the occasion by Sir Hubert Parry, who received a baronetcy in the Coronation Honours List.

The service proceeded much as it had for centuries, although there had been some concessions made to aid the King in his physical recovery. Instead of the traditional St Edward's Crown, in use since 1661, he was crowned with the much lighter Imperial State Crown – this had been used for his then 19-year-old mother, in 1838. In addition, Randall Davidson, the Bishop of Winchester, altered the service slightly to keep it as brief as possible, while retaining its spiritual character.

Towards the end of the service there was some concern when the King did not emerge from St Edward's Chapel – where the royal couple had changed into their robes – until some ten minutes after his wife. Worries were soon put aside when, in the words of William T. Stead, the controversial newspaper editor who would later perish on the *Titanic*, 'He held his sceptres firmly and walked with steady steps down the Nave.'

The coronation of Edward VII was the first to be filmed. The British Mutoscope and Biograph Company captured some of the procession. Two clips survive: one showing the military participants; the other the King and Queen in their carriage, both captured from the same spot.

There is also a fragment of a ten-minute film made by Mitchell and Kenyon showing a second procession which had been planned to tour the City of London and Southwark the day after the service, but was postponed until 25 October because of the King's health.

No film cameras, however, were permitted inside the Abbey for fear of the noise disturbing proceedings. In fact, without the installation of special lighting, the Abbey's interior would have been far too dark for the fledgling technology to film. However, for those keen to see what the ceremony looked like, French filmmaking pioneer George Méliès had produced *Le Sacre d'Édouard VII*, filmed in France, and which premiered on Coronation Day. Méliès was famous for his reconstructed newsreels of major events, as well as for his *A Trip to the Moon* fantasy piece. He chose his cast according to their physical similarity to their real-life counterparts. Queen Alexandra was portrayed by an actress from the Théâtre du Châtelet, while the King was played by attendant from a suburban Paris washhouse.

What no film managed to capture was the long list of mishaps that took place during the real ceremony. Frederick Temple, the 80-year-old Archbishop of Canterbury, was in frail health yet insisted on putting duty first. He refused to delegate any part of the ceremony. His failing eyesight meant that he struggled to read the prayers, despite them being printed in large type onto 'prompt scrolls'. He then almost dropped the crown and placed it on the King's head back-to-front. After paying homage to the King, Temple could not rise to his feet and had to be helped up by the King and several bishops. Much of the congregation heard him loudly scold an unfortunate colleague who asked after his wellbeing with the words 'Go away'. But it wasn't just ageing clergy who disrupted proceedings. The King's own sister, Princess Beatrice, dropped her service book from the gallery to a table below, where it landed rather noisily, startling everyone. Even the King himself caused quite a stir when he responded to the Prince of Wales's traditional gesture of homage – touching the crown and kissing his father's left cheek – by rising to his feet and throwing his arms around his son's neck in a surprising public show of affection.

According to *Lloyd's Weekly*, unfortunate incidents were not confined to inside the Abbey, nor even London itself. At 9 am in The Mall, a carriage carrying Lord Edward Pelham-Clinton, Master of the Queen's Household, had collided with an empty carriage travelling at high speed towards Buckingham Palace. Although the collision was not too serious, the horses were clearly shaken and began to kick violently. Police in attendance had to rescue the startled passenger and untangle the horses – a lengthy task because the animals continued to panic. Worse was to come. At around 4pm a horse attached to a carriage picking up a coronation guest in Whitehall bolted then collided with another carriage which overturned, crashing into 'six native Indian troopers [one of whom had been knocked unconscious], a woman and a policeman', who were all taken to Westminster Hospital with injuries that included 'concussion of the brain', three fractured skulls, broken bones, severe scalp wounds, and various cuts and bruises.

Most of those needing medical treatment in London were victims of 'fatigue and excitement', but outside the capital, as well as a number of incidents of trips and falls during celebrations, there were two very serious incidents. One took place at Blackpool Winter Gardens where two attendants, named only as 'Nolan and Higham', were firing the coronation salute when there was an unexpected misfiring. Both men sustained serious facial injuries. Newspapers across the county informed readers: 'Nolan is expected to lose his sight, his face being mutilated beyond recognition'.

Then there was the tragic case of 37-year-old David Hewitt of North Walsham in Norfolk. He had been in the process of firing an old cannon at Westwick Park when 'the weapon exploded with disastrous results'. Both his hands were blown off and his face and head severely injured. He was taken immediately to hospital, but died the following day. It was later concluded that, despite having been given some instruction earlier in the day on how to safely operate the cannon, he had failed to clear out all the smouldering residue before attempting to fire it again, causing a premature explosion.

Back in London, celebrations continued as the King and Queen appeared on the balcony of Buckingham Palace to greet the crowds – continuing a precedent set by his mother during the opening of the Great Exhibition in 1851.

That evening a reassuring medical bulletin was issued stating that the King had coped well with the physical stress of the day. Most importantly, according to *The Times* at least:

> King Edward is the first of our kings to be attended in his coronation by an illustrious group of statesmen from our self-governing colonies, as he is the first to be accompanied by a number of the great feudatory Princes of India ... They are bound to preserve the fabric of British polity and of British civilisation.

CHAPTER 5

Establishing Modern Britain

> There are so many in the country blessed by Providence with great wealth, and if there are amongst them men who grudge out of their riches a fair contribution towards the less fortunate of their fellow-countrymen they are very shabby rich men.
>
> David Lloyd George, Limehouse Speech,
> 30 July 1909, London.

The Second Boer War and the First World War would become the bookends that defined the limits of the Edwardian era. Yet neither conflict would dominate the political scene in the twelve intervening years.

Instead, consecutive governments, generally holding only light grasps on power, would wrestle with renegotiations of the relationship with Britain's closest continental neighbour, and the complex question of how Ireland could be governed. And then there were thorny issues of domestic reforms in education, the criminal justice system, workers' rights, and the beginning of the creation of a welfare state. Dominating all of that was the debate over just how these reforms could be afforded. How the bill would be paid. And how an agreement could be reached between capitalist and socialist interests.

Lord Salisbury's Conservative government had been elected in 1895. And re-elected with a landslide in 1900 in a patriotic campaign that had pitched Liberal criticism of the Boer War – not just that it was being fought badly but that it was being fought at all – and Conservative assertions that a vote for the Liberals was, essentially, a vote for the Boers. In 1902, with the Boer War won and a new monarch settled on the throne, the 72-year-old Salisbury found himself widowed and in poor health, and decided to bring his long political career to an end. He proposed that his nephew, Arthur Balfour, succeed him.

Balfour continued on the path of his predecessor. His first significant success was the passing of the Education Act 1902.

Often known as the 'Balfour Act' – since he had drafted and introduced the Bill while still serving in Salisbury's government – it created Local Education Authorities to run English schools in place of local school boards, and a controlled secondary education system.

Like any revolutionary idea it met considerable opposition, particularly from Methodists, Baptists and other Nonconformist groups who were irritated at the loss of their influence on school boards while, they claimed, Anglican and Catholic schools were being supported.

Secondary education was now available only in designated secondary schools. Councils were encouraged, but not compelled, to help fund free places for working-class children in existing grammar schools, and to establish new secondary grammar schools. However, the slow roll-out of that part of the measures meant that, initially at least, secondary schools concentrated on providing for middle-class pupils.

The Liberal Party, whose supporters included large proportions of Nonconformist voters, led the opposition to the Bill. In protest, there was a mass withholding of rates payments. By 1904 more than 37,000 summonses for unpaid school taxes had been issued. The Education Act proved so controversial that it is credited for the Liberals' unexpectedly large election victory of 1906. The Liberals then attempted to introduce an Education Bill of their own to correct what they believed to be the unfairness of the Balfour Act. This proposed state control of all voluntary schools, including church schools, and proved even more unpopular. Catholics objected to state control of their schools, Anglicans to the teaching of non-denominational worship, and Nonconformists to the teaching of denominational worship in state schools.

There was now a debate over whether it was appropriate, or even possible, for the state to control a privately owned school without confiscating its property. Every attempt – of which there were many – to please an opposing lobby group seemed only to aggravate the others. The second Bill was introduced to the Commons on 9 April 1906, but when it reached the Lords it inevitably became entombed in numerous amendments. Repeated attempts to pass it failed and it was finally withdrawn. Somehow, from the position of Leader of the Opposition, Balfour had managed to keep his own Education Act intact, without a single amendment.

In 1906 and 1907, the Liberals did manage to pass Bills to further provision for the general welfare of children. The Education (Provision of Meals) Act allowed – although again, did not enforce – local authorities to provide meals free of charge when parents could not afford to pay. The Education (Administrative Provisions) Act required education authorities to provide all children under its care with a medical inspection.

On the international stage, Balfour's most important contribution was the Entente Cordiale, or 'friendly understanding', with France with whom Britain had a number of long-running disagreements. Importantly, on 8 April 1904, four key agreements (notably, not treaties) were declared. The first, and perhaps most important, was a declaration respecting Egypt and Morocco. While France recognised Britain's position in Egypt, Britain did the same for France in Morocco. Free passage through the Suez Canal was guaranteed, and France agreed not to erect fortifications on the Moroccan coast, threatening passage through the Straits of Gibraltar.

The second agreement concerned fishing rights in Newfoundland and West and Central Africa. France agreed to renounce fishing privileges in Newfoundland in return for Britain compensating French citizens for that loss while, in return for territorial concessions in West and Central Africa, France retained the right to fish on the former French Shore 'on a footing of equality with British subjects'. In addition, agreements were made over interests in Asia – specifically Siam (Thailand), Madagascar and New Hebrides (Vanuatu). The agreement was generally regarded as a great success. Most importantly, the Entente Cordiale paved the way for Franco-British cooperation in the face of German agitation in the decade that would precede the First World War.

In 1905, Balfour found himself in an internal party battle over tariffs versus free trade. Unable to keep a successful balance he resigned as Prime Minister in the hope that Liberal leader Henry Campbell-Bannerman would be unable to form a strong enough government. However, when the King invited the Liberal leader to form a minority government, he accepted and immediately called a General Election, which the Liberals won with a large majority.

Campbell-Bannerman became the first person to be officially named Prime Minister, rather than First Lord of the Treasury. He was not able to enjoy that position for long. In 1908, following a sudden deterioration in his health, Campbell-Bannerman resigned and was replaced by Herbert Henry Asquith. Familiarly known as 'H.H.', the new Prime Minister was to discover quite quickly the difficulties of passing radical legislation through a House of Lords loaded with Conservatives, while the Lords were to discover that Asquith at least matched them in stubbornness and political guile.

On 29 April 1909, Asquith's Chancellor of the Exchequer, David Lloyd George, introduced his so-called 'People's Budget'. A budget that he argued would eliminate poverty, declaring:

> This is a war budget. It is for raising money to wage implacable warfare against poverty and squalidness. I cannot help hoping and believing that before this generation has passed away, we shall have advanced a great step towards that good time, when poverty, and the wretchedness and human degradation which always follows in its camp, will be as remote to the people of this country as the wolves which once infested its forests.

It was intended, he said, 'to cope with the social condition of the people, to remove the national degradation of slums and widespread poverty and destitution in a land glittering with wealth'.

Lloyd George's goal was to produce a budget that would not only improve Britain's military defences in the face of German armament, but would also pay for Asquith's new social reforms which would mark the beginning of the welfare state. There were plans to open Labour Exchanges across the country, provide for a degree of unemployment insurance in certain trades such as building and mechanical engineering, and to introduce National Insurance to provide sick pay and medical treatment for workers. But this could come only at a cost and the method of raising funds for this, and the expansion of Britain's military defences, were to prove extremely contentious. An expansion of the Royal Navy, with new 'dreadnought' battleships, was estimated at £3 million. But the introduction of an old-age pension for the over 70s would cost the public purse more than £8 million. In total, Lloyd George estimated that there would soon be a shortfall of around £16–17 million. And he knew just how it could be afforded.

A radical overhaul of the nation's finances was required. Lloyd George's solution was to produce what is widely regarded as the first modern budget – one which would significantly redistribute portions of the nation's wealth. He declared, 'I made up my mind, in framing the Budget which was in front of me, that at any rate no cupboard should be barer, no lot would be harder. By that test I challenge them to judge the Budget.'

Indeed, that Budget ensured that the richest members of the society would foot the bill. Measures were carefully targeted to protect all but the richest. Basic income tax on earned incomes was only to be paid by those earning more than £160 per year – most working men did not reach that threshold – and held at 9d in the pound. For those earning above £2,000 – only 25,000 individuals – this was raised to one shilling, and for those earning over £5,000 – some 10,000 individuals – it was 6d in the pound on any income over £3,000. Death duties were also increased, licences were introduced for motor cars, and there was a 3d per gallon levy on petrol. For those who were middle or working class there was little reason to object. For example, for those earning less than £500 per year – which covered the majority of the middle classes – Lloyd George introduced £10 tax relief for every child under

16 years of age. Those most able to afford it were now going to support those in the greatest need.

Most Conservatives, however, believed that the traditional methods to raise funds were better. The placing of tariffs on goods imported from outside the Empire would benefit British industry and could also be arranged to promote trade between Empire territories. In fact this would have raised prices on all imported food, and any benefit gained by British manufacturers and producers would have been far outweighed by the cost to ordinary consumers.

The People's Budget also introduced a series of new land taxes. All land was to be valued and a 20 per cent tax levied on any increase in value when the land changed hands. Unsurprisingly, with a House of Lords filled with the nation's largest landowners, this met with immediate and strong opposition. But it was not just Conservatives that opposed it. Liberal Lords like former Prime Minister Lord Rosebery also objected. Ironically, it had been his Chancellor of the Exchequer, Sir William Harcourt, who had introduced controversial death duties in a budget of 1894. That did not stop him denouncing the People's Budget as 'pure socialism'. Lloyd George and his great ally – the 34-year-old President of the Board of Trade, Winston Churchill – became known by critics as the 'Terrible Twins'. The Liberal majority ensured that the Budget passed through the Commons with little problem, but the Lords threatened to veto it.

Although they were entitled to reject a budget, no House of Lords had done so for two centuries. This was a worrying constitutional development. Privately, the King urged the Lords to pass the Budget and avoid a crisis. But, on 30 November 1909, they vetoed it regardless, although they did agree that the budget would be passed once the Liberals had achieved an electoral mandate for it. In return, the Liberals threatened to reduce the power of the Lords, and so the policies on which the General Election of January 1910 was fought were set. Although it returned a hung parliament, the Liberals maintained control, thanks to the cooperation of the Labour Party and the Irish Parliamentary Party. As promised, the Lords passed the People's Budget on 28 April 1910.

But the Commons and Lords were still at odds and a second General Election was held in December 1910, again returning a hung parliament. Asquith was now determined to weaken the Lords' stranglehold on Parliament.

For months the Prime Minister had attempted to persuade the King to ennoble a large number of Liberals – several hundred of them – to shift the balance in the Lords, but Edward had refused, stating that he would only consider this after a second General Election. Edward died in early May, just days after the Budget had passed, bringing his son, George V, to the throne. At first Asquith was reluctant to ask the new king to intervene, but had eventually all but forced his hand by suggesting that the entire Cabinet would resign if the monarch did not agree. George V wrote in his diary, 'I disliked having to do this very much, but agreed that this was the only alternative to the Cabinet resigning, which at this moment would be disastrous.'

To prevent the Lords from blocking future legislation, and so hamstringing Parliament whenever it had the fancy, Asquith brought in the Parliament Act (1911) which removed the power of the House of Lords to reject Bills dealing with money, and to replace their veto with the power of delay of two years, after which a law could be passed by the Commons alone. The Parliament Act passed through the Commons but, inevitably, was heavily amended by the Lords. Asquith told the King that it was time to create the new Liberal peers, and the King agreed, provided that his intention be made public, so that the Lords be given time to reconsider their position. After weeks of debate, the Conservative peers, realising the futility of their situation, agreed to allow the Bill to pass and the Parliament Act went through the Lords by a 131–114 majority in August 1911. It had taken time, but Asquith's careful and clever manoeuvring had worked – he had, effectively, altered the way constitutional matters operated and put the elected house in control. But even that would not solve all the trickiest political issues of the early twentieth century.

The question of Ireland was a particularly complex one which had preoccupied many governments. The Irish nationalist movement was long established. Since the 1870s, calls for Irish Home Rule – self-government within the United Kingdom of Great Britain and

Ireland – had been most prominent. Gladstone's Liberal government had introduced the First Home Rule Bill in 1886, but it proved contentious – not least within his own party – and was defeated in the Commons. Another attempt in 1893 passed the Commons, but was defeated by the Lords.

The Conservative Government introduced reforms to Ireland that it hoped would kill off any interest in Home Rule. Balfour's government's Land Purchase Act of 1903 instigated the greatest social revolution in Ireland since the seventeenth century. The Act encouraged Anglo-Irish landowners to sell off their land to their tenants who could secure a loan from the Government to make the purchase. Loans were to be paid back over 68.5 years at 3.75 per cent interest. Compensation was paid to landlords, and the purchase price of land was calculated by multiplying previous rent with a specified number of years. Annuities due represented a significant reduction on previous rents.

Precise totals were agreed between landlord and tenant and were approved by the Estates Commissioners. A further Act, in 1909, tweaked the terms and offered greater compensation for landlords, while reducing the repayment period to sixty-six years at a rate of 3.5 per cent. In total, just shy of 11 million acres over thirty-two Irish counties were sold to tenants running approximately 320,000 holdings, or 60 per cent of them. But the question of Home Rule remained.

Despite the large Commons majority that the Liberals enjoyed from 1906, even enthusiastic supporters of Home Rule realised that the anti-Home Rule majority in the Lords was simply too great to pass such a law, so little progress could be made. After the passing of the Parliament Act in August 1911, a third Home Rule Bill was introduced. It was anticipated that even without the support of the Lords it could pass into law by the end of 1914 at the latest. The Unionists were angry, accusing the Liberals of entering into a deal with the Irish Parliamentary Party simply to push through Home Rule, even though it had not been part of the Liberals' election manifesto. Thus began a coordinated effort to prevent it becoming law, which attracted 447,205 Ulster Unionist signatories to a covenant and declaration opposing it. At the same time 100,000 Unionists joined the Ulster Volunteer Force, although commitment to the paramilitary group was varied. Training sessions were sometimes poorly attended and within the UVF there were both peaceful and militant elements. When it became clear that the Unionists were not simply going to accept Home Rule, the possibility of partitioning part, or all, of Ulster – where Protestants and Unionists tended to live – was discussed. By spring 1914, with the Government considering using the military to enforce Home Rule, some sixty army officers, from 3rd Cavalry Brigade declared that they would rather resign their commissions than be forced to act against the Ulster Volunteers. It became clear that other officers were in sympathy, and so the idea of using the British Army to counter the UVF came to an end. As the situation became more acute, King George V called the leaders to a conference at Buckingham Palace, without any agreement being reached.

As it transpired, the outbreak of war, in August 1914, would calm matters – at least for the time being. Within two years, however, Britain would be more urgently revisiting the 'Irish Question'.

CHAPTER 6

BROKEN BONES BETTER THAN BROKEN PROMISES

> The argument of the broken pane of glass is the most valuable argument in modern politics.
>
> Emmeline Pankhurst, *Votes for Women*,
> 23 February 1912.

In the early evening of Friday, 1 March 1912, the streets of London's West End descended into chaos when around 150 Suffragettes from across the country, women from all backgrounds and of all ages, converged on the capital and, armed with toffee hammers, clubs and stones, began breaking the windows of some of the city's most high-profile shops and offices.

The events of that evening shocked a nation. And yet they could hardly have come as a surprise. To anyone even casually observing the campaign for women's suffrage, it had been clear for some time that the patience of the 'Votes for Women' lobby was wearing thin. Campaigners felt that they had nothing left except to take increasingly extreme action. Yet it might have been so different.

The struggle for a woman's right to vote was one of the most contentious issues of the Edwardian Era. But the battle for women's suffrage had been fought for far longer. Most years between 1870 and 1884 had seen Parliamentary debates held on the matter. Millicent Fawcett, the sister of Dr Elizabeth Garrett Anderson – the first officially qualified female British medical doctor – was 50 years old when she formed the National Union of

Women's Suffrage Societies (NUWSS) in 1897. The widow of the radical Liberal MP Henry Fawcett was attempting to coalesce the many small groups that had been established around the country.

Fawcett was frustrated by the disparities she saw. For example, of the disenfranchised women who ran businesses and thus controlled the working lives of men who were entitled to vote, even though many of them were less educated than the women who employed them. It was a point she made with some regularity to those who claimed to doubt female ability to understand Parliamentary processes.

The NUWSS campaigned, held public meetings, organised petitions and lobbied for the vote to be extended to women. Their tactics were considered and decidedly peaceful. While they wanted to improve women's rights, they believed that rocking the Establishment to its foundations was not the way to achieve their aim. Gradually, their tactics were changing minds and garnering influential supporters. Before long the organisation had an estimated 100,000 members.

Suffragist meetings were held regularly up and down the country. In May 1901, Birkenhead and Wirral Women's Suffrage Society held a 'drawing-room meeting' at the home of the mayoress at which the principal speaker, Mrs Allan Bright, tabled a resolution that 'In the opinion of this meeting the exclusion of women ratepayers from the Parliamentary franchise is unjust to them and detrimental to the best interests of the country.' She complained, also, that the lack of representation meant that laws which might be to the benefit of women simply did not get drawn-up or passed. She cited the case of the 'Deceased Wife's Sister Bill', designed to permit a widowed man to marry his late wife's sister. In contrast, there was no equivalent 'Deceased Husband's Brother Bill', permitting a widow to marry their brother-in-law.

Another speaker, Hope Rea, voiced the widely held concern that the greatest danger to women's rights came from those who felt that now several acts of Parliament had been passed to 'improve' the lot of women, there was less reason to push through legislation to grant them the vote. Indeed, quite the opposite was true, because those 'privileges' were granted by the grace of men and could be taken away at will, without women having any say in the matter.

While many suffragists believed that it was only a matter of time before they succeeded, there were others frustrated at the painfully slow rate of progress. Among them were Emmeline Pankhurst and her daughters, Christabel, Sylvia and Adela. In 1903 they formed the Women's Social and Political Union (WSPU) and took a decidedly less patient, more militant approach to their cause, taking up the motto 'Deeds Not Words'.

They were far more vocal, less apologetic, and demanded attention. Almost immediately they attracted criticism. Opponents sought to paint the women as immature. Anti-suffrage postcards were produced depicting them as mewling babies demanding their vote. Or calling their leader 'Miss Ortobee Spankdfirst'. Others were equally offensive and patronising – and not really all that clever, with images of men dressed in women's clothing, a deliberate conflation of wanting equal rights with men, with actually wanting to be men. They were accused, too, of wanting to dominate men in every walk of life, and were reminded that they would be better occupied in taking care of their children and homes. But, rather than inflicting ridicule, the tactic damaged the anti-suffrage cause and gave previously apathetic women encouragement to speak out.

In contrast to the stereotype ridiculed in the newspapers, WSPU members went out of their way to appear smart and stylish at all times. In 1908 they adopted something of a 'uniform', and official colours of purple 'for dignity', white for 'purity' and green for 'hope' were adopted. The colours had been chosen by Emmeline Pethick-Lawrence, treasurer of the WSPU and co-editor of *Votes for Women* magazine, which advised:

> If every individual in this union would do her part, the colours would become the reigning fashion. And, strange as it may seem, nothing would so help to popularise the WSPU ... now everyone has simply got to see to it that everywhere our colours may be in evidence.

The WSPU campaign of direct action had begun in 1905. They interrupted political meetings, made public protests, raised banners and placards.

When, the following year, Charles E. Hands of the *Daily Mail*, began to refer to the WSPU as 'Suffragettes' – a nickname clearly intended to belittle the group – it gave them a title to rally behind. And it served to distinguish between the WSPU and the NUWSS. Because there was no doubt that while their cause was the same, their methods were becoming entirely different. The Suffragettes enthusiastically adopted their new nickname and even titled their newspaper in its honour. By February 1906, the WSPU was known, almost exclusively, as Suffragettes.

During the General Election of 1906, which saw the Liberals under Henry Campbell-Bannerman victorious, both groups had campaigned enthusiastically, but were generally seen as an incidental nuisance. The *Folkestone Express, Sandgate, Shorncliffe and Hythe Advertiser* noted that 'very little attention was paid to their speeches or manifestoes ... many people are inclined to think that they have already rather too much political influence than too little'.

The Suffragettes were about to demand more attention. In May 1906, what the *Sheffield Evening Telegraph* called 'an orderly, neatly attired little band of about 50 women of all ages', each representing a trade union from Lancashire or Cheshire, gathered in London. They were joined by colleagues from Bromley and Poplar. Other groups arrived every few minutes and a procession formed up, bound for Whitehall.

While there were many trades union banners, the most notable were the 'proliferation' of banners bearing the words 'WE DEMAND THE VOTE THIS SESSION'. Most dominant, though, was the large red banner from the WSPU which proclaimed, 'WE DEMAND VOTES FOR WOMEN'.

Accompanied by a number of bands, the long procession made its way past the end of Downing Street, stopping as it reached the Foreign Office. There the women addressed the new Prime Minister, who listened as various representatives complained that their 'crushing exclusion' from suffrage impacted on their wages and their status, argued that there was no logical reason for their exclusion, and reminded him that men were not the only breadwinners. The sympathetic Campbell-Bannerman agreed that they had made good points, and asked only that they exercised some patience. When the women made clear their irritation, he advised them that since the tide of public opinion was clearly now turning in their favour, they would be best advised not to do anything controversial. 'The deputation expressed themselves very dissatisfied', noted the *Sheffield Evening Telegraph*.

If the women suspected delaying tactics, they would soon be proved right. Suffragists campaigns were expanding, but little progress was being made. In February 1907, the NUWSS organised the peaceful United Procession of Women in London, at which more than 3,000 women marched from Hyde Park Corner to The Strand – despite the unrelenting heavy winter rain which left participants drenched and so splattered with dirt, that it became known as the 'Mud March'. The march did not change anything politically, but it was widely reported, and it was now clear to both suffragist movements that the way forward must include more mass public gatherings and meetings on this scale.

On 21 June 1908, the WSPU organised Women's Sunday – a huge march and rally held in the capital. It attracted a remarkable number of supporters – an estimated half a million – from all over the country, many of whom who were greeted at London's railway stations and escorted to the gathering by marshals and stewards. Some 30,000 women, carrying 700 banners, marched to Hyde Park in seven processions. Ten thousand Suffragette scarves had been sold, and male supporters were encouraged to wear ties in WSPU colours. A host of famous faces joined the event, including politician Keir Hardie, Irish playwright George Bernard Shaw, and novelists H.G. Wells and Thomas Hardy.

Although the NUWSS and WSPU already had very different methods, the two groups were initially supportive of each other, even when the latter began chaining themselves to public buildings. In October 1908, two Suffragettes chained themselves to a grating inside the Ladies' Gallery at the House of Commons. They shouted, 'Votes for Women!' and a portion of the grating had to be removed to extricate them. As the second of the women was removed to a nearby committee room, a shout came from the other side of the Chamber as a man, this time standing in the Strangers' Gallery, shouted, 'I demand justice for the women of England!' and threw a sheaf of leaflets into the Chamber. Another man then followed suit. Both were removed. Chaos ensued as every woman present was then suspected of being a Suffragette and was also removed from the gallery which was then closed. Outside Parliament a crowd managed to force its way inside as far as St Stephen's Hall before being blocked from the Lobby. Eleven Suffragettes were jailed for their actions that day. One of those arrested was Emmeline Pankhurst who was imprisoned after being found guilty of issuing leaflets encouraging her supporters to 'rush the House of Commons'.

Millicent Fawcett wrote a letter to *The Times* in support of the women:

> The real responsibility for these sensational methods lies with the politicians, misnamed statesmen, who will not attend to a demand for justice until it is accompanied by some form of violence. Every kind of insult and abuse is hurled at the women who have adopted these methods, especially by the 'reptile' press. But I hope the more old-fashioned suffragists will stand by them; and I take this opportunity of saying that in my opinion, far from having injured the movement, they have done more during the last twelve months to bring it within the region of practical politics than we have been able to accomplish in the same number of years.

Encouraged by the publicity that their actions were generating, the WSPU turned to more noticeable tactics. In April 1909, four women chained themselves to statues inside St Stephen's Hall. In June, Marion Wallace-Dunlop stencilled a passage of the Bill of Rights on the wall there. Imprisoned, she became the first Suffragette to go on hunger-strike, a tactic that would become a key element of the campaign. Eventually, so many of the women joined in that the authorities took the decision to try to strap them into a chair and force-feed them. It was a particularly brutal, torturous and dangerous process – and one that proved entirely ineffective. The hunger-strikers continued until they neared the point of serious illness. The authorities, fearing the creation of martyrs to the Suffragette cause, should any of the women manage to starve themselves to death, introduced the Prisoners Temporary Discharge for Ill-Health

Act. This allowed the release of the hunger-strikers until their health recovered, at which point they could be re-arrested and imprisoned again, beginning the cycle once more. It became known as the 'Cat and Mouse Act'.

While suffragists found support across the country, in many towns they also encountered vocal opposition. In November 1909, Christabel Pankhurst arrived in Derby to address a meeting at the Drill Hall, where she was met by several angry men who invaded the platform to prevent her speaking. Christabel, however, was unbowed, returning twice to the town in the following few weeks, each time finding less and less resistance to her cause. By the time Emmeline attended the same venue the following April, she was able to hold a peaceful and productive meeting.

On the face of it, progress towards women's suffrage was being made – but then it stalled, election promises were broken, and everything changed.

During the run-up to the General Election of January 1910, the suffragists had been assured by new Liberal Prime Minister H.H. Asquith, who had taken over from an ailing Campbell-Bannerman, that should his party retain power, then women's voting rights, albeit in limited form, would be properly addressed. Some, though, had doubted that Asquith, always a vocal anti-suffragist, would keep his word. Despite a Cabinet that contained several supporters, they were right to be cynical. Indeed, over the next three years, three separate so-called Conciliation Bills which had appeared to be proceeding through parliament were suddenly thwarted.

The 1910 Bill passed its second reading on 11 and 12 July, despite a number of notable MPs, including David Lloyd George and Winston Churchill (whose opinion on the subject seemed to change with the tide) voting against it. In 1910, Churchill, a Liberal at the time, was of the mind that granting women the vote was somehow 'anti-democratic'.

Regardless, the election had seen Asquith ruling a minority government. Come November there was an impasse between the Commons and Lords over the controversial People's Budget and Asquith called another General Election and the Conciliation Bill was dropped entirely.

On the day this was announced, the WSPU was holding a widely publicised rally at Caxton Hall in Westminster, with a demonstration planned for later that day. When news reached the meeting, a deputation of around 300 members, divided into small groups, began to walk to Parliament where they hoped to meet with Asquith in person. The first group, which included Dr Elizabeth Garrett Anderson and Princess Sophia Duleep Singh (daughter of a deposed maharajah and goddaughter of Queen Victoria), were told that the Prime Minister would not meet with them. They were escorted outside where things would soon get out of hand. That day the usual 'A' Division of police, who had become familiar with the WSPU, had been replaced with officers from Whitechapel and the East End, heightening tensions.

The precise details of what occurred that day are difficult to discern, such are the differing accounts. But events quickly became ugly. As the next group of Suffragettes reached Parliament, they encountered a group of men, possibly plain-clothed policemen, who pushed and manhandled them and shouted insults of a sexual nature. Over a spell of some six hours, later arrivals were intercepted by uniformed officers, roughed up and then pushed into the hostile crowd of male onlookers and subjected to further assault. The Suffragettes had set up a medical rest area at Caxton Hall. Sylvia Pankhurst recorded, 'We saw the women go out and return exhausted, with black eyes, bleeding noses, bruises, sprains, and dislocations. The cry went around, "Be careful; they are dragging women down the side streets!" We knew this always meant greater ill-usage.'

One of those taken into a side street was Rosa May Billinghurst, a childhood victim of polio and a wheelchair user who, after being assaulted by police, had the valves taken from her chair's wheels, leaving her unable to move.

One hundred and fifteen women, and four men, were arrested that day. But none faced trial. Home Secretary Churchill decreed that there was 'no public advantage' in prosecuting and all charges were dropped. At the same time, he declined to investigate all claims of police brutality. The following day, few newspapers mentioned any hint of police ill-doing, although they covered what they called 'Black Friday' at length and in great detail. The *Daily Mirror* did feature a photograph of a Suffragette lying on the ground, having been struck by a policeman. When the newspaper put the photograph to the police commissioner, he claimed the woman had collapsed from exhaustion. Twice, calls for a public inquiry were rejected by Churchill. Regardless, journalist Henry Brailsford and psychotherapist Jessie Murray gathered 135 statements from demonstrators, some twenty-nine of which featured disturbing allegations of sexual violence by police, in the form of pinching, wringing and nipping of breasts, and pushing themselves towards the bodies of the women. Often this had taken place in full public view to ensure as much humiliation as possible. There would also be claims that two Suffragettes had died due to their treatment on Black Friday. Emmeline Pankhurst's own sister, 48-year-old Mary Clarke, had been present that day. On 11 November she was arrested for breaking windows in Downing Street and sent to prison for a month. She died on Christmas Day of a brain haemorrhage. Emmeline believed firmly that this was due to the actions of police at the November protest.

Henria Leech Williams had travelled to the Black Friday protest from Upminster. She gave evidence on her treatment by police that day:

> One policeman, after knocking me about for a considerable time, finally took hold of me with his great strong hand like iron just over my heart. He hurt me so much that at first, I had not the voice power to tell him what he was doing. But I knew that unless I made a strong effort to do so, he would kill me. So, collecting all the power of my being, I commanded him to take his hand off my heart. Yet that policeman would not arrest me, and he was the third or fourth who had knocked me about. The two, first after pinching my arms, kicking my feet, and squeezing and hurting me in different ways, made me think that at last they had arrested me ... but they each finally took me to the edge of the thick crowd, and then, without mercy, forced me into the midst of it, and with the crowd pushing in the opposite direction for a few minutes I doubted if I could keep my consciousness,

and my breath had gone long before they finally left me in the crowd ... Finally, I was so exhausted that I could not go out again with the last batch that same evening. Although I had no limbs broken, still my arms, sides, and ankles were sore for days afterwards. But that was not so bad as the inward shaking and exhaustion I felt.

She also reported that one 'gentleman', Frank Whitty, had rescued her from the mob three times. He would later write, in a letter published in the WSPU newsletter *Votes For Women*,

> I saw ... sights that made me feel ashamed of my country; one of the cruellest cases was that of a brave lady ... in a semi-fainting condition, so much so that she could hardly stand. Time after time, with a courage that should have shamed the police into doing their obvious duty and arresting her, she attempted to get through the cordon. I went to her side to do what I could to help and uphold her in her brave but hopeless struggle. At first I tried to persuade her to leave the crowd [but] ... realised her determination to 'do or die' ... All I could do was to try and help her to the best of my power and to ward off the blows, kicks and insults as I could from her fainting body ... Time after time we were forced back into the crowd by the police with an amount of violence and brutality entirely unnecessary. On these occasions I had to put my arm around her to keep her from falling under the feet of the horses, or worse still, under the crowd.

On 2 January 1911, Henria Leech Williams died. The coroner ruled her death was due to 'angina pectoris'. Comments in the press suggested that perhaps a woman with a weak heart ought not to participate in Suffragette activities. Her fellow activists, however, were quite certain that the blame lay squarely with the police. Her brother, Llewellyn, believed her to be a martyr. 'She knowingly and willingly shortened her days in rendering services to the womanhood of the nation.'

When shown Brailsford and Murray's report, Churchill acknowledged in Parliament the nature of some of the allegations, yet declared, 'If there were any truth in them, they should have been made at the time and not after a lapse of three months.' After all, the Home Secretary had been reassured by the Commissioner that the allegations were 'devoid of foundation'.

Whatever elements had combined to cause the deaths, the appalling events of Black Friday were the catalysts that altered the WSPU's tactics. Tired of being overlooked and pushed to one side, they now turned to something that could not be ignored – the large-scale destruction of property.

Although Suffragettes still thought up inventive and non-criminal ways of disrupting public meetings and appearances by notable politicians – like those in Sheffield who managed to several times interrupt Winston Churchill's appearance at the city's Cutler's Hall by sending the guest of honour a number of telegrams during the event – they would now concentrate on criminal damage.

As Emmeline Pankhurst was to write: 'The argument of the broken pane of glass is the most valuable argument in modern politics.'

In early 1912 the WSPU set out plans for a 'Great Militant Protest' for the weekend of 1–4 March. This was to culminate in what invitations would call a 'Great Protest Meeting' on the evening of Monday 4th. Secretly, something more headline-grabbing was being organised, the full extent of which would not become clear until they unfolded on London's streets. As an estimated 150 Suffragettes descended on London late on Friday afternoon, the authorities became aware that something was afoot. Special Branch officers waited outside the Gardenia Restaurant on Catherine Street in Covent Garden, inside of which Suffragettes were being briefed and given small weapons.

Plain-clothed officers had been deployed at various points identified as likely targets for Suffragette activity. But the women were not wielding their weapons openly. And there were plenty of others strolling around in small groups, who were in the capital for entirely innocent purposes.

The Suffragettes' aim, after all, was not to get away with their acts of criminal damage, but to take their punishment with pride. Each woman was well aware of the consequences of her actions. And the risk to her personal safety, reputation and liberty. In evidence later used at the trial of Emmeline Pankhurst for conspiracy, Lilian Ball, a dressmaker, married with three children – one of them just 4 years old – told police that she had been asked by an unidentified organiser whether she was 'prepared for a long or short sentence'. She had answered, 'A short one, as I had made arrangements for absence from home for seven days.' Told to choose a small window at the United Service Museum to break, she was given a small hammer with the words 'Better Broken Windows Than Broken Promises' written on it. Ball was advised to conceal the weapon up her sleeve until the appropriate time. 'She told me I shouldn't have more than seven days if I only broke one small pane.' It must have been a shock, then, when, after her conviction for doing damage worth three shillings, Ball received a sentence of two months' hard labour in Holloway Prison.

When the window-breaking began, it began quickly, without warning, and in so many places at once that despite their preparations, the police were still overwhelmed.

As readers of the *Northampton Chronicle* would learn the following day, events had begun shortly after 5pm with an attack on Downing Street. A private motor car containing Emmeline Pankhurst, Emily Marshall and Mabel Tuke had pulled up outside No. 10:

> Immediately a crash of glass was heard and before the police knew what was happening, four windows on the ground floor of Mr Asquith's house had been smashed by the occupants of the car. Three women were promptly arrested and taken to Cannon Row Police Station where they were subsequently charged was causing wilful damage in company with six other Suffragettes.

Police managed to arrest several women quickly. Alice Wilson was seen throwing a stone at a ground-floor window in Whitehall. Three more women were followed to the post office on the King's Road where they were observed smashing a window. Windows across London came under attack, but it was those on The Strand, Cockspur Street, The Haymarket, Piccadilly, Regent Street, Bond Street, Conduit Street, Oxford Circus, Oxford Street and Coventry Street that bore the brunt. Newspapers blamed the action on 'bands of hysterical women'.

Late into Friday night, as calm was restored, London's shopping streets echoed to the sound of nails being hammered into wood as damaged windows were boarded up. The *Northampton Chronicle* noted, 'London resembled in many parts a barricaded city … At 8.30 the Strand from Charing Cross to Fleet Street was lined with police … Double patrols were placed outside most of the unfortunate shops and private detectives were also on duty at various points.'

In total, 126 women faced trial, receiving prison sentences ranging from fourteen days to six months. All but fifty also received hard labour. The sheer scale and intensity of the action certainly came as a shock and was strongly criticised in the mainstream press.

On Sunday, 10 March 1912, *Lloyd's Weekly* noted, 'The determination of the leaders of the militant section of the women's suffrage movement in this country to continue the policy of violence, as destructive in its effects as it is illogical and illegal, has clearly alienated a considerable amount of sympathy from the general cause.'

But the WSPU were making their point and there now followed more than two years of increasingly militant action. There were numerous instances of window smashing and other small acts of criminal damage – or direct action, depending on your point of view. Paintings and other works of art were attacked. At the Hertfordshire town of Potters Bar in September 1912, trunk telegraph wires were cut, and in November there were simultaneous attacks on post boxes across the country. By the end of 1912 some 240 women had been imprisoned for Suffragette militancy. And so it continued.

On 10 February 1913, three orchard houses at Kew Gardens were attacked overnight with windows smashed and flowers scattered around. An envelope labelled 'Votes for women' was left at the scene. The following month a fire was set at the Tea Pavilion in the early hours of the morning.

As the attacks increased, so did the criticism of the movement in the local press. The *Derby Daily Express* urged the 'shaving of the heads of every militant Suffragette'. It was a stance that an increasing number of people in that particular area were to take. In 1911, Edward Mundy of Shipley Hall had built a 300-yard (274m) wall around his property to protect it from what he saw as the Suffragette threat.

Of course, in order to make their point it was important that the WSPU be connected with each act. But this also meant that soon every unattributed act of violence or vandalism was blamed on Suffragettes. And there must have been instances that were either the work of someone else for an entirely different purpose, or a deliberate attempt to besmirch the Suffragettes. In Derby, one incident in particular would stain the Suffragettes' reputation for some time to come.

On the night of 5 June 1914, the 900-year-old church of All Saints' at Breadsall, just to the north of Derby, was set alight. Mr Hopkins, a local farm labourer, noticed a flickering glow through a window and hurried to awaken the verger, Mr E. Endsor, who was also the village postmaster. By the time they and the rector, Oxford graduate Reverend John Ayton Whitaker, and two churchwardens, Colonel W. Beadon Woodforde and Mr H. Buckingham, arrived on the scene, the church was fully ablaze. Red tape caused more delay. The nearest motorised fire engine was in Derby, and permission had to be sought from the chairman of the local Watch Committee before that could be summoned. By the time the engine arrived at the church everything but the tower and spire was beyond saving.

By morning there was only one group of suspects. Reverend Whitaker told a *Derby Daily Telegraph* reporter, 'It has been done by Suffragettes, I know it has.' Whitaker called the Suffragettes 'mad women'. Evidence showed that it had been an arson attack, but nothing remained to identify the perpetrators, and there was no note claiming responsibility. The only piece of evidence at the church itself was the discovery of a hatpin close to a broken window through which it was assumed the arsonist had gained access. That a parishioner might have innocently lost the hatpin was not considered for long because the small hole had been adjudged particularly suitable for use by a woman. Reverend Whitaker announced that he expected they would soon receive a note claiming responsibility and sure enough, a few days, later a card arrived bearing the words 'Let there be light. The price of liberty. Votes for Women', accompanied by a page from *The Suffragette*. Might this have been confirmation? Or simply the work of an agitator keen to further tarnish Suffragette reputation? Now rumour and circumstantial evidence swirled around the village, but descriptions of people allegedly seen loitering in the churchyard varied so much that they were of little use. The only direct link to the Suffragettes were the words 'Votes for Women' chalked on a wall a mile away, and such political graffiti was hardly unusual. As controversial as the Breadsall fire was, no one had been harmed. And that was not always the case.

Even activities such as the destruction of the contents of post boxes was difficult to dismiss as victimless when at least one postman reported burns to his hands after coming into contact with sulphuric acid that had been poured into the pillar box he was emptying. There had also been occasional close calls when members of the public had narrowly escaped one of the arson attacks on buildings that were not quite as 'empty' as initially thought. And when the Suffragettes began a new, explosive, campaign, which caused even greater damage, the risk to the general public increased considerably.

There were, of course, those Suffragettes who disagreed with some of the more extreme tactics. Twenty-two-year-old Theresa Garnett, for instance, who brandished a whip at Winston Churchill during his visit to Bristol, gate-crashed a Foreign Office reception to mark the birthday of Edward VII, and was accused of biting and kicking a prison wardress, yet still left the WSPU in protest over its arson campaign. Garnett, who had once put a match to her prison cell, drew the line at setting alight public buildings.

The question of whether the Suffragette bombing campaign of 1912–14 constituted terrorism is a thorny one, particularly since it is now universally accepted in modern civilised countries that a woman's right to vote is sacrosanct. There is absolutely no doubt that the Suffragette cause was worthy. How reasonable were their actions remains open to debate. The movement as a whole targeted property and not people. And yet, inevitably, there were injuries, some of them serious. The campaign most certainly spread a great deal of fear across the population. Some of the more extreme examples might well fall under modern anti-terrorism laws. But terrorism itself did not exist in law in Edwardian times, and most bomb-planters were prosecuted under the Malicious Damage Act 1861.

The campaign began in Dublin, on 19 July 1912 – the same day as a bomb was discovered at the office of Home Secretary Reginald McKenna – at Dublin's Theatre Royal where Prime Minister Asquith was due to attend a performance. The women struck at the end of the first show, as the audience was leaving the theatre. Gladys Evans, Lizzie Baker, Mabel Capper and Mary Leigh attempted to set a fire. Petrol and lit matches were thrown into the projection booth, and a canister of gunpowder was set close to the stage. Mary Leigh, who earlier in the day had hurled a hatchet at Asquith but narrowly missed him, would later state that Suffragettes were under instruction not to harm any living thing. The authorities thought otherwise and all four were charged with offences likely to endanger life. It was the first 'terrorist' bomb planted in Ireland in the twentieth century.

Suffragettes were also responsible for some of the first letter bombs. On 6 February 1913, five Dundee postal workers were burned, four severely, when handling a Suffragette letter bomb addressed to Asquith. In May, a parcel bomb containing gunpowder and nitro-glycerine was discovered at Borough Market Post Office in London, and nine days later a similar device, intended for the anti-suffrage barrister and politician Sir Henry Curtis-Bennett, was planted in Bow Street.

Then, on 2 June, a large letter bomb was discovered at London's South Eastern District Post Office. Had it exploded, reports suggested it contained enough nitro-glycerine to blow up the whole building and kill the entire workforce of 200.

On 26 June, in the Welsh town of Caerleon, Margaret Mackworth posted a letter in a pillar box. A short time later the box began to smoulder and caught fire. Margaret was arrested. Given the option of a fine of £10 with £10 costs, or one month's imprisonment, she chose the latter. Although she was a leading member of the Monmouthshire WSPU, newspapers largely preferred to define her by the terms of her relationships with the men in the life, calling her 'the daughter of a wealthy "coal king"', and the wife of Captain Humphrey Mackworth 'the heir to a baronetcy'.

July proved a busy month in the campaign. On the 5th there was another near miss, this time at Bolton's Spinner's Hall, when a package containing gunpowder was put through a letterbox. The fuse went out when the bomb landed on a tiled floor. Three days later, a bomb was placed on the counter of Blackburn's main post office but again was discovered before it could explode. Three days after that a railway guard suffered severe burns to his arms after trying to throw a burning letter bomb from a moving train in Salwick on the Preston–Blackpool line.

In February 1913 a house being built for Chancellor of the Exchequer, David Lloyd George, was the target of two bombs, only one of which exploded. And a year later a bomb exploded at the home of Arthur Chamberlain, brother of Joseph Chamberlain, in Moor Hall Green, Birmingham.

With so many bombs being laid in so many places, it was inevitable that members of the public would be put at risk. The driver of a passenger train passing by Stockport was nearly killed when a bomb placed beside the tracks exploded, sending debris flying. And passengers on a train travelling from Waterloo to Kingston were caught up in a fire when one of two bombs laid by the line detonated. There was a plot to destroy the grandstand at the Crystal Palace football ground on the eve of the 1913 FA Cup Final between Aston Villa and Sunderland.

More and more dangerous and damaging devices were used, like the pipe bomb set off at Newcastle Crown Court in April 1913, and the one discovered at St Paul's Cathedral which was packed with shrapnel to do maximum damage. Another such device was discovered in the waiting room at Liverpool Street Station on 10 May. Unfortunately, on 11 June 1914, a bomb, packed with nuts and bolts, did explode at Westminster Abbey causing significant damage to the ancient Coronation Chair and breaking the Stone of Scone in half. Remarkably, none of the eighty or so people in the Abbey at the time were harmed. As the device went off, next door MPs were debating the best means of dealing with the Suffragettes.

Vital infrastructure was considered a legitimate target. In January 1914, a powerful bomb exploded at the Crown Point Electricity Generating

Station in Leeds, causing much damage. In June 1913, an explosion on the Stratford-upon-Avon Canal at Yardley Wood, Birmingham, caused serious damage. It could have been so much worse – had the banks burst, the breach would have emptied all the section's water on to the populated valley below. A month later, a device was discovered on the Brock Aqueduct in Manchester, which took the main line of the Lancaster Canal over the natural waterway. In May 1914, an attempt was made to flood a populated area by planting a bomb beside a large reservoir near Penistone in South Yorkshire, which contained 630 million litres of water – part of the supply for several towns and villages.

A report in *The Sheffield Daily Independent* suggested:

> If the water of the reservoir had been released by the explosion it would have swept with terrific force on to the village of Dunford Bridge at the foot of the valley and poured into the Great Central main line, possibly flooding Woodhead Tunnel.

The same month, two bombs were discovered at the Glasgow Aqueduct and another at Glasgow Water Works with the assumed intention of cutting off the city's water supply.

Such violent and extreme tactics resulted in a loss of support for the WSPU by those unwilling to publicly link themselves with such potential atrocities. It also hardened opposition. Such was the backlash against Suffragettes that simply being associated with the cause became something of a risk. But one incident in rural Wales stands out for its extraordinary brutality and violence.

On 22 September 1913, David Lloyd George was to give a speech in Llanystumdwy, the village in which he had grown up. Before he could begin, the first of a group of Suffragettes began calling out for 'Votes for Women'. According to the *Daily Mirror*:

> At once pandemonium reigned, and hundreds of Welshmen rushed at a luckless Suffragette. Catching hold of her by the waist, they dragged her away from the crowd and maltreated

her. Her hat was torn away, and armed with cabbage stumps and sticks the crowd struck the unfortunate woman on the head, in the face and on other parts of her body. Meanwhile the policeman – there were twenty-four – and three plain-clothed detectives fought hard to give her protection. Their efforts were useless, as the gathering was nothing but a mass of howling men mad with anger. One man forced his way through the dense mass to where the police were trying to get the fainting woman away. Laughing and waving his hands, he struck her a terrible blow to the jaw. This stunned her, and she was then conveyed to a cottage, a howling crowd following her and her two protectors.

As the police carried her away, Lloyd George called for calm and resumed his speech. Four more Suffragettes then called out. They were met with even more fury and force:

One woman was stripped to the waist, and one man pulled a bunch of her hair out and boastfully waved it to the view of those around him. As the second of the four women was heavily thrown to the ground and then lifted, ultimately being thrown into the middle of a ditch on her back. The crowd took the opportunity of throwing missiles at her as she lay. A rush was made for her when she had recovered her feet, and she was half carried and half dragged to Llanystumdwy bridge, the intention being to throw her over into the river. Had she gone over the parapet she would have been killed by striking the boulders studding the shallow riverbed.

Fortunately, the police had realised the mob's intent and managed to prise the Suffragette away from her attackers and take her to safety. Few in the village gave any shelter to the women. When one was spotted hiding on the stairs of a cottage, she managed to shut the door just in time and a mob surrounded the building and had almost managed to force their way inside when truncheon-wielding police came to the rescue.

On occasion, members of the more peaceful NUWSS were subjected to mistreatment by members of the public unable, or unwilling, to differentiate between militant and non-militant campaigners. In early August 1913, Catherine E. Marshall of the NUWSS (which had by now adopted red, white and green as its official colours) had written to Home Secretary Reginald McKenna, requesting a meeting. A recent five-week 'Pilgrimage' organised by the NUWSS had seen members taking one of six main marching routes to London, passing through towns and villages as they went, spreading the word and holding meetings and rallies.

This had culminated in a large rally at Hyde Park on 2 August where the crowd was addressed by Millicent Fawcett herself. According to Marshall, in several places along the route the police had failed to protect the 'pilgrims' from the wrath of sometimes hostile members of the public. Marshall assured the Home Secretary that these hostilities were from a minority of those they met, and had the 'organised hooliganism being more promptly checked by the police' there would have been no issue. She complained at the lack of legal redress for women like 'Miss Margaret Ashton, of Manchester City Council [who] can be stoned in the public streets with impunity, whereas, had she been a plate glass window, the offender would be severely punished'.

McKenna replied that, while his immediate responsibility was limited to the Metropolitan Police, he accepted that it was 'only fair' that suffragists receive as much protection as other citizens.

> If there is any impression that women's suffrage meetings are 'fair game for the mob' we will do our utmost to remove that impression and give you protection ... on the other hand, it would be reasonable to expect that if meetings are held which ... are not viewed favourably by a certain rowdy section ... the police should get full notice of your intentions and that you should take their advice as to the places and times at which meetings should be held ... I shall certainly do my utmost to ensure that there is absolute fair play for both sides ... I am sure these gangs of roughs of which you ... justly complain are just as obnoxious to me as

other persons ... who endeavour to enforce their opinions in a way which I can only regard as being of the same kind of actions as roughs. You and I have a common duty in this. You desire, as I do, to enforce political opinions and action by constitutional methods and if I may express an opinion I honestly and sincerely believe that your method of action has assisted your cause and, although I do not share your views, I am convinced that your methods will be infinitely more successful in achieving your wishes than the methods of an opposite kind ... I should like to add that I sincerely admire the courage with which you ladies have carried on your work and I assure you that you shall have the fullest protection which is the undeniable right of every law-abiding subject.

All this aside, members of the WSPU in particular were not going to be distracted from the cause by risks to their personal safety. A stance that would result in the most famous event in British women's suffrage history.

Emily Wilding Davison, the 34-year-old governess to the children of Sir Francis Layland-Barratt MP, joined the WSPU in 1906. Eighteen months later she resigned from her job to become one of the most enthusiastic activists. In a period of just over five years she was arrested multiple times, imprisoned eight times, and participated in seven hunger-strikes. She had written to then Home Secretary Herbert Gladstone (son of former Prime Minister William Gladstone) warning, 'Ours is a bloodless revolution but a determined one [we are] ready to suffer, to die if need be, but we demand justice!'

A determined and well-educated woman, Davison had been forced to abandon her studies at (what is now Royal) Holloway College when her father had died. Taking on enough work to fund her own studies at St Hugh's Hall, Oxford, she passed her examinations with first-class honours in English Language and Literature, but was unable to acquire a degree, since Oxford awarded only male graduates the honour. Undeterred she then studied at London University, which did award degrees to women, and this time graduated with honours in classics and mathematics. Nevertheless, like every other woman, however well educated, she faced limited employment opportunities.

In addition to taking direct action, Emily wrote a number of articles in support of the cause. What would be her last – 'The Price of Liberty' – was published in the *Daily Sketch* on 28 May 1913 and used dramatic language: 'The perfect Amazon is she who will sacrifice all … to win the Pearl of Freedom for her sex. Some of the bounteous pearls that women sell to obtain freedom … are the pearls of friendship, love and even life itself.'

One week later, Emily Davison arrived at Epsom racecourse on Derby Day, purchased a race card and made her way to the side of the track, squeezing in beside the rails ready for the biggest race of all to start at 3pm. What she was about to do had probably not been planned for long. She had originally arranged to spend the day at the Suffragette Fair and Festival at the Empress Rooms in Kensington, but the day before she began discussing with fellow sympathisers the possibility of staging a protest at the racecourse. While no official plan was made, Emily had already formulated one of her own. The next morning, as she left the Lambeth home of Alice Green, she pinned a Suffragette flag inside her jacket, took her purse, a few coins and stamps, a notebook, her key and a Suffragette sash which she concealed inside a sleeve. She took a tram to Victoria and purchased her return train ticket for Epsom Downs. The course was packed with racing enthusiasts from all walks of life. Ordinary punters mixed with high society enthusiasts. Also present were King George V – whose horse, Anmer, was a Derby runner – and Queen Mary.

At three o'clock, fifteen horses set off. Fifteen horses running at full pelt for glory over one mile and four furlongs. By the time the race reached Emily's position, Anmer had fallen back to the trailing pack. Once the leaders had stormed past, Emily pulled out her sash and dipped under the rails. Calmly she made her way out on to the track, while all about her was sound and motion. She held her hands and sash high and appeared to step towards Anmer.

We will never know her true intention. Had she not realised that not all the horses had passed by? Did she want, perhaps, to raise her colours in the wake of the runners and in full view of the watching crowd? Or did she intend to sacrifice herself? To cause a collision with a horse? Did she even know, at that point, that the horse she stood before belonged to the king? Recent forensic analysis of several angles of film footage poses another possibility – that Emily sought simply to reach out to a horse – the king's horse – and drape a Suffragette sash over its head or saddle. It would certainly have been quite a coup. Whatever her intention, and despite jockey Bertie Jones's considerable efforts to pull Anmer away, there was a horrific collision and Emily was sent flying.

According to the *Daily Mirror*, 'The horse struck the woman with its chest, knocking her down among the flying hoofs ... and she was desperately injured ... Blood rushed from her mouth and nose. Anmer turned a complete somersault and fell upon his jockey who was seriously injured.'

Remarkably, it transpired that Anmer had been only slightly injured and was fit enough to race at Royal Ascot two weeks later – ridden by Jones, who had recovered from his concussion. But Emily, called in a letter by Queen Alexandra, 'a brutal lunatic woman', suffered catastrophic injuries and died a few days later in the local cottage hospital.

It is probably fair to assume that Emily had not intended her actions to have fatal consequences. Many have cited her purchase of a return ticket as proof that she intended to return home, but it was the only type of ticket on sale that day. More compelling were her other personal effects: a ticket to a Suffragette dance later that day, and a diary full of appointments for the following week.

The Suffragettes had their martyr. Others would use Emily Davison's actions as proof that women could not be trusted with the vote. Lord Curzon – a lifelong opponent of women's suffrage – claimed that the Suffragettes 'have rendered us the service of showing how easily disturbed the mental balance of some women, at any rate, can be'.

And therein lay the problem. The more militant the act, the more it laid the Suffragettes open to accusations of behaving irrationally. This was seized upon by those already opposed to granting women the vote. And there was no doubt that many who supported the principle of women's suffrage found it impossible to wholeheartedly support the WSPU itself. The particular question of whether a Bill to grant women the vote would have proceeded through Parliament more quickly had the WSPU not resorted to its bombing campaign is impossible to answer. Potentially, it might have. Although the governments of the time had shown reluctance to get on with the legislation, almost every year since 1867, at least one Private Member's Bill had been proposed. But without the cooperation of government, these Bills could never get beyond the first reading. And then, in 1914, came the possibility, then reality, of war in Europe, and any such idea was moved aside for the foreseeable future. The WSPU continued its bombing campaign to the end, with the last bomb exploding in Lisburn, Ireland, on 1 August 1914, calling a halt to its actions the moment war was declared. Emmeline and Christabel Pankhurst believed that it would be highly unpatriotic to continue the disruption at such a moment. Sylvia Pankhurst, however, was very much opposed to the war and denounced it.

The Representation of the People Act 1918 would pass through the House of Commons on 19 June 1917, by a majority of 385 to 55. It extended the vote to all men over the age of 21, and to women over the age of 30 with land or property with a rateable value above £5, or whose husbands did. The General Election of 1918 was the first election under the new rules. In 1928, the franchise was extended to all women over the age of 21.

CHAPTER 7

CRIMES AND PUNISHMENT

> Take the case of a young man who, in an erring moment, falls victim to some vice which warrants arrest … incarcerated for a week with the vilest of the vile, the scum of the city … [his] spirit is broken, his reputation gone, his sense of honour blasted.
>
> *Dundee Courier*,
> 30 December 1907

At the end of Queen Victoria's reign, Britain was policed by 181 independent territorial forces, compared to forty-five today. And although the nation had a total of 60,000 police officers, more than three dozen forces each employed less than fifty officers, and there was little cooperation between forces, each having its own way of working.

Now, with an increasingly mobile population, it became important that forces began to work together. Yet, as attitudes to crime, punishment and offenders began to change, the crime rate during Edward's reign, perhaps influenced by better social standards and an overall reduction in poverty, was lower than during that of his mother's.

The Gladstone Report of 1895 concluded that prisoners should leave prison better people than when they went in. The purpose of imprisonment now changed from one of harsh punishment to one of reform. The attitude to younger criminals also changed. A report from the Prisons Committee in 1894 had drawn particular attention to the treatment of young offenders – a group that it believed was being neglected and allowed to fall under the influence of older and more hardened career criminals.

The Pall Mall Gazette of 22 October 1902 explained to its readers the thinking behind suggested reforms:

> In this country when a lad over 16 commits an offence, reformatories and industrial schools are closed to him, and if he is deprived of his liberty at all, it must be within the walls of a prison.
>
> All the available evidence goes to show that the effects of this system have been disastrous ... experts in English criminology are generally agreed that it is between the ages of 16 and 21 that the habitual criminal is formed – a process greatly facilitated by the fatuous habit of giving short sentences – and a recent census of those of the penal servitude population may be described as 'professionals' revealed the fact that nearly half of them were under 21 on first conviction ... The bulk of our young criminals are ordinary lads ... whom it behoves the State to try to rescue before they reach the social ruin of penal servitude.

Children were held separately from adults, but once they reached the age of 16 they were introduced to the standard prison system. The report recommended raising the age of entry to reformatories from 16 to 18, and that for detention to 21.

An experimental 'special class' had been created at Bedford Prison. The lads held there had been taught a trade, given special training and supervised and guided after their release. So improved had been their outcomes that what would be known as the Borstal school system – after the prison school at which it was first established – was started in 1902 with the intention of reforming wayward youngsters into useful members of society. Inmates were classified into one of three groups: penal, ordinary and special. Each group was kept separate from the others and wore a different uniform. Each inmate would rise through those classes at a speed determined by their 'industry and good conduct', and adversely affected by any 'idleness or misconduct'. All inmates were 'employed in association in workshops or in outdoor work, such as farming ... and they shall be instructed in useful trades and industries which may fit them to earn their livelihood on release'. The more dramatic their reform, the quicker they could be released – some as early as six months into their sentence, while others remained in the system for two years.

Daily exercise and education formed an important part of any sentence. Lectures and 'moral addresses' were given, and the inmates had access to library books and 'useful literature' which they were encouraged to read. And, prior to their release, arrangements were made with Discharge Prisoners' Aid or 'other philanthropic societies or benevolent persons'.

This change in the perception of children from being subservient to being protected, and encouraged to become important and responsible members of society, was reflected in the work of Robert Baden-Powell in his creation in 1908 of the Boy Scouts, and the Girl Guides the following year. The year 1908 would also prove important in the legal protection of children. The Children and Young Persons Act came into effect, introducing a set of regulations known as the Children's Charter. Designed to protect children from cruelty, it required the registration of all foster parents, imposed severe punishments on those neglecting or mistreating children, and made it illegal to sell cigarettes to children, give them alcohol while under the age of 5 (unless for medicinal purposes), to send them out begging or to allow them to enter brothels or the bars of pubs.

Also from 1908 youth and adult criminal justice was separated further when special juvenile courts were established, with their own set of procedures and punishments.

This more compassionate approach was also seen as a means to reduce reoffending and, effectively, cut off a ready supply of recruits to the professional criminal classes.

In 1898, Captain David Dewar, the chief constable of Dundee's police force, had introduced a probation system into his courts – police were generally responsible for detecting, investigating and also prosecuting crimes, and Dewar was also procurator-fiscal for the city. He believed that many offenders, when given the chance and suitable guidance, would readily become law-abiding citizens. With the help of local charitable agencies and the Salvation Army, he established a scheme in which offenders of less serious crimes, first-time offenders, and those where there were extenuating circumstances, were given the opportunity to take a six-week period of supervision. Since many crimes were deemed to be alcohol-related, probationers were encouraged to take the pledge of abstinence. At the end of that time conduct was reassessed and they were either 'admonished' or 'punished'.

The scheme was so successful, with a 90 per cent rate of success, that other towns and cities across Britain chose to establish their own system. Before long a national scheme was introduced.

The Probation of Offenders Act 1907 did not establish a probation system in the modern sense. Instead, it gave judges the means by which they could dismiss a charge against a defendant if they believed that the defendant's character, age, physical or mental health, extenuating circumstances, or the trivial nature of the charge, warranted it. Others who were willing or able to pay a contribution to charity, repay the costs of stolen goods, or compensate for the costs of what they had done, could also be 'given the Probation Act' without being convicted of a criminal act. Instead, magistrates' courts appointed probation officers, paid for by the local authority, to 'advise, assist and befriend' those under their supervision.

As the national attitude to crime changed, so the public of Edwardian Britain could rely less upon sensational crimes and trials for their entertainment gained through often lurid newspaper reports and magazine articles.

But there would still be those crimes and subsequent criminal trials so extraordinary that public fascination was guaranteed. The case of Hawley Harvey Crippen, the American medical man who stood accused of the murder of his wife, was just such a case.

Although known as 'Doctor Crippen', he was not licensed to work as such in the United Kingdom. His qualifications, as a homeopath and ear and eye specialist, had been earned in the United States. Crippen moved to London in 1897, with his second wife, Cora – whose aspirations, under the stage name Belle Elmore, to become an acclaimed music hall singer floundered due to her mediocrity – to manage the British office of a homeopathic company and was often referred to in newspaper reports as a 'dentist'.

It was not a happy marriage and both husband and wife had affairs – Cora with one of the lodgers at their home at 39 Hilldrop Crescent in London's Holloway, and Crippen with one of his employees, Ethel le Neve. To the outside world, the Crippens presented a happy picture, but on the evening of 31 January 1910, when they held a party at their home, guests witnessed a tiff between the couple. That night was the last time that Cora was seen alive.

In the weeks that followed, Dr Crippen's name would occasionally appear in entertainment trade journals – *The Music Hall Theatre Review* and *The Stage* among them – in connection with financial donations he had made to theatrical organisations. No suspicions were raised. No concerns were aired. Until, that is, his wife's friends became worried for the welfare of Cora. No one had seen her for weeks and only four weeks after the last sighting, Ethel le Neve had moved into the Hilldrop Crescent house, and had begun openly wearing Cora's clothes and jewellery, even at social occasions that she and Crippen attended together. Over a short time, Crippen told a developing story that, following the January party, Cora had returned to the United States, had become ill and had unexpectedly died. But strongwoman Kate 'Vulcana' Williams, and actress Lil Hawthorne and her husband John Nash, were unconvinced and reported Cora's disappearance to the police. A search of the house found nothing suspicious, and Chief Inspector Walter Dew (who had also been involved in the hunt for Jack the Ripper) accepted Crippen's new version of events – that his wife had not died but had left him and returned to the US with one of her lovers. And that could have been that. But Crippen did not know that his explanation had been so readily believed. He feared that he was still under suspicion. He and Ethel fled London in a panic. Their sudden flight rekindled suspicions and brought the police back to the house where a new search proved more fruitful.

Using the eye-catching headline 'London Murder Mystery ... Police Story of Strange Crime ... wanted man seen in Kingsway – said to have gone away with his typist', the *London Evening News* reported: 'Late last night there was found in the cellar of the house the remains of a woman, which the police believe to be those of Cora Crippen. Her husband ... is wanted for "murder and mutilation".'

What had actually been found was the remains of the torso of a female, so mutilated that it was little more than flesh. There was no head and no bones.

As the hunt for Crippen and le Neve began, Scotland Yard issued detailed descriptions of the pair. Crippen was:

> Age 50, height 5ft 3in, complexion fresh, hair light brown, inclined sandy, scanty and bald on top, long sandy moustache, rather straggly ... may be clean shaven or wearing beard, eyes grey, flat on bridge of nose, false teeth, wears gold-rimmed spectacles ... rather slovenly appearance, throws his feet out when walking, speaks with slight American accent, wears hat back of head. Very plausible and quiet spoken, speaks French, carried firearms, shows his teeth very much when talking.

Ethel Le Neve was 27, 'height 5ft 3inches, complexion pale, hair light brown, large grey eyes, good teeth, good looking, medium build, pleasant appearance, quiet, subdued manner. Looks intently when in conversation, walks slowly, reticent ... native of London. Shorthand writer and typist.'

Crippen and le Neve, who was disguised as Crippen's son, had already gone into hiding and, on 20 July 1910, the pair boarded the SS *Montrose* at Antwerp. They were bound for Canada.

Had Crippen and le Neve travelled third class then they might not have been recognised. But the ship's captain, Henry Kendall, recognised them from the Scotland Yard descriptions and sent a wireless telegram reporting: 'Have strong suspicions that Crippen London cellar murderer and accomplice are among saloon passengers. Moustache taken off, growing beard. Accomplice dressed as boy. Manner and build undoubtedly a girl.' Chief Inspector Dew travelled to Liverpool to board the faster White Star's SS *Laurentic* for Quebec. He arrived there ahead of the fugitives and informed the authorities.

While, on 30 July, British newspaper readers learned that the pair had been located and would soon be arrested, the lovers continued their charade. The following day, as SS *Montrose* entered the St Lawrence River, Dew boarded disguised as a harbour pilot. The pair were arrested and returned to Britain – since Canada was a British dominion, there was no need for any extradition proceedings.

Crippen's four-day trial took place in October 1910 at the Old Bailey, the new building which had been opened on the site of the old Newgate Prison three years earlier. Pathologists testified that, without limbs or a head, it was difficult to identify the deceased, but one of them, Bernard Spilsbury, said that he had found an identifying scar on the abdominal skin of the torso consistent with Cora's medical history.

The defence argued that since the Crippens had only occupied the house from 1905, the torso might easily have been buried by a previous occupant. However, a scrap of fabric from a pyjama top was found beside the remains. It matched a pair of bottoms found in Crippen's bedroom and was found to have come from a fabric not on sale prior to 1908, putting it in the correct timeframe for the Crippens' residence.

Crippen, who had maintained his innocence throughout, and showed no concern for his wife, only for his lover's reputation, was found guilty.

Le Neve, tried for being an accessory to murder, was successfully defended by F.E. Smith, who would become one of the most famous and highly paid barristers of his generation and who would later be ennobled as Earl of Birkenhead.

Hawley Harvey Crippen, the first criminal to have been apprehended through the use of wireless telegram, was hanged at Pentonville Prison on 23 November 1910. He was buried in the prison grounds with a photograph of Ethel le Neve.

CHAPTER 8

DEPLORABLE SACRIFICES OF HUMAN LIFE

> I am afraid we must brace ourselves to confront one of those terrible events in the order of Providence which baffle foresight, which appal the imagination and make us realise the inadequacy of words to do justice to what we feel.
>
> Prime Minister Asquith,
> 16 April 1912

The self-confidence that Britain enjoyed during the Edwardian era took a devastating blow in what would be one of the defining moments of the early twentieth century. The sinking of the 'practically unsinkable' RMS *Titanic* – at 46,328 tons the largest liner in the world – in the North Atlantic in April 1912 came as a terrible shock to a public that had, thus far, been fascinated only by the ship's top-class facilities and VIP passenger list.

One of those first-class passengers, the Philadelphia-born John Borland 'Jack' Thayer III, was 17 when he boarded the *Titanic* with his parents and their maid, Margaret Fleming, at Cherbourg on 10 April 1912. Young Jack's father perished, while the youth, his mother and their maid survived.

Twenty-eight years later – and five years before he took his own life – Jack Thayer wrote about life before and after the sinking. In a 1940 self-published pamphlet he said:

> It seems to me that the disaster about to occur was the event that not only made the world rub its eyes and awake but woke

it with a start, keeping it moving at a rapidly accelerating pace ever since with less and less peace, satisfaction and happiness. To my mind the world of today awoke April 15th, 1912.

For the first few days after the White Star Liner left Southampton, much had been written about the enormous size of the vessel, of the passenger accommodation, in particular, of the elegance of the First Class facilities and the unusually well-appointed Third Class areas. There was no steerage on *Titanic* – Third Class passengers slept in larger, shared cabins, albeit in the harder-to-reach areas of the ship, and had their own areas of deck on which to take fresh air and exercise.

Readers were informed that there was a first-class dining room capable of serving 500 passengers at a time. And two miles of deck to stroll on. That a typical cross-Atlantic voyage on the *Titanic* would require 1,500 gallons of fresh milk and 40 tons of potatoes. That meals would be served from some 25,000 pieces of china. And that the fare would cost £7 for Third Class (£800 in today's money), rising to £30 (£3,300) for First Class.

Contemporary accounts of just how many passengers were aboard *Titanic* on her maiden voyage vary. Some did not take into account additional passengers taken aboard at Cherbourg, others seemed to assume an almost full ship. In fact, with good fortune, *Titanic* was well below capacity. Approximately 1,300 passengers were on board – and there were more than 900 crew, making an overall total of around 2,200 souls aboard a vessel that, to many, seemed to encapsulate the Edwardian era.

Briefly, newspaper attention turned to news of the great British explorer Captain Robert Falcon Scott who, it was reported, had reached the South Pole with his small team of explorers. Unfortunately, it was now clear that the British had reached the pole several weeks after the Norwegian Roald Amundsen, but the feat would still 'bring him much fame and honour'. What was not yet known, thanks to the difficulties and extreme delays in communicating with Britain from Antarctica, was that Scott and the rest of his men were dead. Their bodies would be discovered in their tent some eight months later.

Queen Victoria, whose death on 22 January 1901 led to the dawn of the Edwardian Era. (Illustrated London News)

King Edward VII and Queen Alexandra pictured at the State Opening of Parliament in February 1901. (Illustrated London News)

A drawing by Richard Caton Woodville depicting soldiers of C Squadron, 17th Lancers, at the Battle of Modderfontein during the Second Boer War in September 1901. (Illustrated London News)

An advertisement for Bovril published during the Second Boer War. (Illustrated London News)

Procession approaching Leeds Town Hall during the visit of Edward VII to the city in 1908. (Illustrated London News)

Chancellor of the Exchequer David Lloyd George (left) and President of the Board of Trade Winston Churchill, architects of the 'People's Budget' of 1909-10. (Author's collection)

Emmeline Pankhurst is carried away by a police officer after having led a Suffragette protest outside Buckingham Palace. (Author's collection)

An Edwardian dream – 'Dover to Calais by Motor Car and Omnibus'. An artist's vision of a Channel Tunnel, published in *The Sphere* in 1909. (Illustrated London News)

The Hon C. S. Rolls at the wheel of his 80hp Mors racing car with which he held an unofficial land speed record in 1903. (Illustrated London News)

Louis Blériot and his Type XI aeroplane shortly after landing at Northfall Meadow near Dover Castle on the morning of 25 July 1909. Blériot had just become the first person to fly across the English Channel (Illustrated London News).

The Court of Honour at the Imperial International Exhibition at London's White City, staged in 1909. (Valentine' postcard series)

The 'Tudor Village' at the Festival of Empire exhibition held at the Crystal Palace in 1911. The exhibition was postponed on the death of Edward VII and rescheduled to coincide with the coronation of George V. (Valentine postcard series).

Artist's impression of the opening ceremony of the 1908 Olympic Games held at the White City in the presence of Edward VII. (Illustrated London News)

Left: Prince K.S. Ranjitsinhji, one of the greatest batsmen of the 'Golden Age' of cricket, lit up the game during the early Edwardian Era. (Author's collection)

Below: A large crowd enjoying the rowing at Henley was a typical scene during Edwardian summers. (Illustrated London News)

Right: The phonograph, the forerunner of the gramophone, opened up new entertainment possibilities for the better-off Edwardians. (Illustrated London News)

Below: An advertisement for bath salts that seemed to solve all kinds of domestic problems in Edwardian Britain. (Illustrated London News)

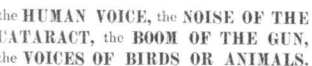

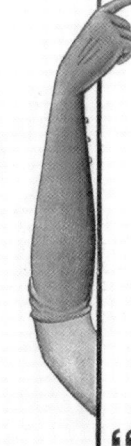

Edwardian ladies' hats grew larger and more ostentatious as the decade progressed. (Illustrated London News)

A raft of new magazines targeted women who often looked to them for advice on the latest fashions. (Illustrated London News)

The barber's shop of Joseph Rippon at High Street, March in Cambridgeshire, pictured in 1906. Five years later his brother, William Rippon, was advertising his 'best in the market' hair restorer from his shop in Spalding. (Author's collection)

A handsome Edwardian couple, insurance agent William Rowley and his wife Jane Eliza, who ran their tobacconist's business in Derby. (Author's collection)

The end of an era. Men from all walks of life crowded into makeshift recruiting offices to fight for King and Country when war was declared in 1914. (Author's collection)

Soon, news of a tragedy much closer to home would bring attention back to *Titanic*. On 15 April, four days into her maiden voyage to New York, came word of the most unthinkable disaster. *Titanic* had collided with an iceberg in the North Atlantic. The first news was sketchy, confusing and often misleading. Several newspapers ran headlines that implied everything was now under control, while the same edition carried reports that this was most definitely not the case. The *Hull Daily Mail* noted that, although the ship was sinking, female passengers were being taken off and placed into lifeboats. And that the liners Olympic, Virginian and Baltic were 'hastening to assist'. The *Liverpool Echo* reassuringly declared: 'No Loss of Life Feared, Passengers All Taken Off.'

The *Yorkshire Telegraph and Star* of that evening also reported the collision, that all passengers had been safely taken off, and even that *Titanic* had restarted her engines and was now bound, albeit slowly, for the safety of Halifax, Nova Scotia, some 300 miles to the north-west. The truth, of course, was very different.

On the lookout for ice all day, and sailing into a moonless night, *Titanic* had hit a large iceberg at 11.40pm. Her first distress call had been received an hour later. Her last transmission was received at 2.10am, just minutes before she foundered. Witnesses on the *Virginia*, which had been receiving communications from the stricken ship, noted that messages had ended abruptly.

But the true horror and scale of the tragedy would emerge only when rescuers arrived on the scene. The nearest help, in the form of the Cunard liner *Carpathia*, arrived too late to save those not already in a lifeboat. And the truth was that there were simply not enough lifeboat spaces for everyone aboard, even with a smaller complement of passengers. There was a plentiful supply of life jackets, which might have saved many more had the ship gone down in more temperate waters. But no one could survive for long that night in the freezing waters of the North Atlantic.

The *Carpathia* arrived at approximately 3.30am – at which point there was little left of *Titanic* save for dozens of lifeboats and a large debris field of flotsam and lifeless bodies. Able Seaman Joseph Scarrott, a survivor of Lifeboat 14, testified at the British enquiry that he remembered 'more bodies than there was wreckage'.

The crew of *Carpathia* worked as fast as they could to take survivors from the lifeboats. But a little over 700 people survived the disaster. More than 1,500 died. In the following days several hundred bodies were plucked from the water by additional ships that came to help the recovery effort.

By the following morning the full extent of the disaster was becoming clear, and newspaper headlines delivered the news in dramatic style. 'Doom of the Titanic' declared the *Leicester Mail*, 'Calamity of the Titanic' said the *Sunderland Daily Echo*. The latter reported, 'Today's messages tell of a calamity unexampled in the history of the mercantile marine.'

Newspapers continued to bring news of the wealthy, and aristocratic, passengers who were lost – characters like millionaires John Jacob Astor and Benjamin Guggenheim – as well as those who survived – like the Countess of Rothes, and White Star's managing director, Bruce Ismay.

For the people of Southampton in particular, the loss of the *Titanic* was an enormously personal event. Some 730 members of the crew had lived in the town. Only 124 survived. More than 500 Southampton households lost at least one member in the tragedy. One street – Malmesbury Road – lost all eight of its men who were working on the ship when she sank.

As terrible as the disaster that befell *Titanic* was, hundreds of thousands of Britons risked their lives every working day during – and, of course, both before and after – the Edwardian era. Coalmining was, by some way, the most dangerous occupation. It was also one that employed the most. In 1913, UK coal production peaked at 316 million tons. (we used 'tons' earlier) Huge numbers of men and boys worked underground, often miles from the safety of the entrance, in dark and dangerous conditions and with the constant threat of volatile coal and its associated toxic gases.

On 14 October 1913, the United Kingdom's worst mining disaster took place at the Universal Colliery in Senghenydd, in the Aber Valley, four miles from Caerphilly, when 439 miners and one rescuer were killed in a massive explosion.

It was not the first tragedy at the mine. In May 1901, eighty-one miners had been killed in a series of three underground explosions. As terrible a tragedy as that was, far worse was to come.

Mines in the area, which produced steam or 'thermal' coal, which was used primarily in boilers, were known to contain high quantities of firedamp – a highly explosive combination of methane and hydrogen. Many would argue that, given the conditions in the mine, and the working practices of the time, a tragedy of this kind was inevitable.

Three hours before the early shift began, firemen went into the pit to begin daily checks for gas. But they had to travel more than two miles from the shaft bottom to reach the workface and, of course, two miles back again. There was simply not enough time to conduct thorough checks, which consisted of placing a naked flame into cavities to see whether the flame lengthened – indicating the presence of gas. The checks quickly completed, between 5.10am and 6.00am, 950 miners descended the shaft for their eight-hour shift.

At just after 8.00am one, possibly two, explosions occurred to the west side of the workings. A subsequent inquiry found that it was most likely caused when a spark from underground signalling equipment ignited firedamp, in turn igniting airborne coal dust and sending a huge shockwave hurtling ahead of the explosion. This caused more coal dust to fly which, in turn, also combusted. The wave travelled up the shaft to the surface where it destroyed the headframe, killed the winder and badly injured his assistant. Multiple fires broke out underground, hampering rescue efforts and trapping miners. Others fell victim to the effects of so-called 'afterdamp' – a poisonous mix of carbon dioxide, carbon monoxide and nitrogen – left behind by the explosion.

When the colliery manager, Edward Shaw, entered the mine he discovered that the 450 men on the east side were unharmed and he ordered their immediate evacuation.

Tackling the fire was problematic. The explosion had fractured the water pipes and Shaw and those survivors who were able had to use hand extinguishers. Within a couple of hours specialist rescue and fire-fighting teams arrived from neighbouring collieries. As did Red Cross and ambulance workers, and a number of police officers brought in by train from Cardiff. Members of the Inspectorate of Mines also arrived to assess the scene. Rescuers worked hard throughout the day and into the night, many risking their own safety. The last survivors were found at 1am.

Throughout the night of 15 October they continued to fight the fire – which blocked access to the rest of the mine – by hand. They worked twenty-minute shifts at a time. Fifty-six bodies were recovered that day. On the 16th it was announced that it was unlikely that anyone else had survived and that the priority would now be to extinguish the fire. Recovery efforts, of course, continued. For two weeks men battled against the fire, which became a less arduous task once a new water supply system was established. Repeated roof collapses and methane leaks caused countless injuries among the workers. One rescuer was killed, and the work was so dangerous that many wrote a precautionary 'last' letter home before going below ground. To reach one part of the now cut-off mine, the rescuers created a new passageway, working carefully with the knowledge that the fire continued to burn below them, while above them there was gas. They knew only too well what would happen were the two to combine.

On 16 and 17 November more than 200 bodies were brought to the surface. Three days later it was announced that 439 miners had died. Many of them had to be identified by their personal effects. Thirty-three men were still unaccounted for. At the end of the month, with eleven of their colleagues still missing, the miners voted to return to work in the eastern section.

The Times noted the trauma on the local community: 'The numbers are truly awful. We talk in awed terms of the decimation of a regiment in a bloody battle, but here a great community engaged in the pursuit of a peaceful vocation is threatened with the loss of at least a quarter of its able-bodied manhood.' Indeed, the deaths of 440 men from such a small community was devastating. Some 542 children lost their fathers, 205 women became widows. Sixty of the victims were younger than 20, eight of them were just 14 years old. In twelve homes a father and a son had been lost; in ten homes two sons were lost; and one 18-year-old girl had lost both her father and a brother and was left to raise her six surviving siblings alone. One woman lost her husband, two sons, a brother and her lodger.

On 23 October, Fenner Brockway, editor of the *Labour Leader*, published a moving and detailed account of his visit to the village and mine four days after the explosion when, in his words, 'The first terrible shock had spent its force. A dull, glazed grief had taken the place of uncontrollable anguish.'

After travelling there on a train packed with the friends and relatives of those who had worked in the mine, he observed one man, James Winstone, as he spoke to his fellow miners gathered on the station platform:

> 'There is no hope, boys,' he says, quietly. They had been saying the same thing themselves, but they bow their heads as they hear what they feared confirmed. Winstone has been in the pit all night, fighting the flames, hewing away through to his imprisoned comrades, struggling for breath in the foul atmosphere. He did not need to tell us. His face was drawn, his eyes were bloodshot, his body limp. And it was not merely physical exhaustion. When he spoke one felt how he had suffered in the sorrow of others.

Brockway described how the rescuers were not the only visitors to the site, and seemed to hint that the village had become a public curiosity: 'The road and the hillside are strewn with pieces of paper, banana skins, and the remnants of food scattered by the thousands of people who have visited the village during the week. Quite near the pit mouth, I see an Italian selling ice cream.'

But Brockway was most struck by the faces of miners:

> One does not often see strong men broken with sorrow. They stand together discussing the disaster calmly and with little evidence of emotion, but the anguish they have gone through is apparent. Few show no signs of tears. They have worked in that pit side-by-side with the men now entombed,

and the horror of the disaster is very real to them. Since the thunder of the explosion first reverberated through the valley and struck terror in their hearts, they have many times lived in imagination the terrible experience of their mates.

Brockway found the blinds of 'every alternate window' drawn, young women, their children tugging at their skirts, standing out on the front waiting for news.

He describes a huge crowd of several hundred people gathered close to the pithead – all of them relatives of the missing.

Brockway ended his piece:

> I know these tragedies are unnecessary. Experts have said so time and time again. When will we take the mines from the coal owners who count dividend of more value than life? Of what worth is our sympathy unless we insist that the miner shall work under the best and safest conditions possible?

It was a sentiment echoed elsewhere in the newspaper, which declared that the Labour movement demanded the same and called upon 'the conscience of the British people' to join them.

A coroner's inquest was held in early January 1914 and returned verdicts of accidental death. A more detailed inquiry took place at the end of the month and ran for thirteen days, during which fifty witnesses were questioned. A subsequent report heavily criticised management practices and the fact that the owners had failed to enact improvements, demanded by the Coal Mines Act of 1911, to the ventilation system that would have enabled them to reverse the direction of airflow and thus blown smoke out through the shaft, which might have saved a hundred lives. However, a counter argument claimed that had the air been reversed, it might have extracted firedamp and directed it into the blaze, causing another explosion. They were also criticised for failures to properly monitor air quality, or remove the build-up of coal dust from the tracks and walkways. Emergency procedures were deemed insufficient with not enough respirators at the mine and an inadequate water supply, especially given that the 1901 accident had proved the mine was prone to fires. Edward Shaw was singled out for criticism. In particular for his decision to wait to call for assistance for at least an hour and a half after the explosion, while he examined the mine himself. While the company was charged with four breaches of the Mines Act 1911, Shaw himself was charged with seventeen. But he escaped lightly. Being found guilty only of failing to keep adequate environmental records and failing to replace a broken lamp locker. He was fined £24 (£2,300 today). The company was fined £10 and £5 5s in costs (around £1,500 today) for the ventilation issues. Given the scale of the disaster, and the devastating human cost, the punishment was hardly punitive. The *Merthyr Pioneer* informed readers this valued a miner's life at 1s 1d (less than £5 at today's value). Although the colliery reopened, it never operated at the same level again. When it was closed in 1928, Edward Shaw was still its manager.

The Senghenydd disaster was all the more shocking because it came less than three years after two similar mining accidents, the first of which took place on 11 May 1910, at Whitehaven. Although the pithead was visible from the cliffs overlooking the town, Wellington Pit extended almost five miles under the Irish Sea. At 7.40pm that day, a loud noise was heard underground, while at the surface a rush of dust-thickened air gushed out of the mine, indicating a probable underground explosion. As the area began to fill with dense smoke and fumes, rescue teams were summoned, but those challenging conditions meant that they did not arrive until 9pm. As the first investigation party entered the mine, hundreds, then thousands, of people from Whitehaven itself had arrived to lend assistance. Fishermen, dockworkers, doctors and nurses, everyone waited to lend a hand in the rescue efforts.

Near midnight two men were brought to the surface; an hour later, two more emerged. The latter pair told rescuers they had been working in a remote area of the pit and, with eleven others, had begun to evacuate when smoke and fumes reached their work area. Only they had managed to force their way out. All four had been working a mile and a half from the explosion, which had occurred three miles out from the shore.

Throughout the night rescuers attempted to reach the furthest parts of the mine but fire and collapses blocked the way, making it impossible to provide fresh air to the many dozens of trapped miners. Frantic attempts to provide a new ventilation shaft were made.

Families of those trapped waited in vigil at the surface, and as time wore on – and party after party of rescue workers returned to the surface to report their lack of success – those waiting for news became ever more distressed.

It was rapidly becoming clear that little could be done while the fires still raged below. To the horror of those waiting, the chief inspector of mines, Mr J.B. Atkinson, gave the order to build a 2ft deep 'stopping' to starve the fire of oxygen. Four days after the explosion, seven men, including the mine manager, two of his assistants and an experienced mine rescuer, entered the mine. They were wearing breathing apparatus which allowed them to continue beyond the 200-yard point at which their canary had fallen from its perch, indicating toxic air. They continued until the smoke thickened to the point where they could no longer see their electric lamps, and the heat became too intense. And they were still 400 yards away from the fire. There could be no more survivors. The decision was made to seal the mine. For the time being, the bodies of 136 missing men and boys would remain unrecovered. Only on 11 September was it finally deemed safe to recover their bodies. Colliery doctor, Dr Harris, recorded that, of the 136 who perished, only twelve had died from the explosion. Most had been killed by carbon monoxide, or other noxious gas poisoning, or by suffocation. Several deaths were due to burns and shock.

Poignantly, it then became clear that, although the men were likely already dead by the time the mine was sealed, some of those who had survived the initial explosion had done so for long enough to leave messages behind. Notes written in chalk on doors gave details of the men and where they were. One, written on a piece of wood found near to several bodies, stated, 'All's well in this airway at 4 o'clock. 35 men and boys.' It was signed 'J. Moore' and was later identified to be the work of James Moore, who died with his brother in the pit.

Even as that community struggled to return to normality another, even worse, tragedy struck. Four days before Christmas 1910, what was to prove the nation's third worst mining accident happened at Westhoughton in Lancashire in which 344 men and boys died.

Approximately 900 miners had arrived for their day's work at Hulton Colliery Bank Pit No 3 – known as the Pretoria Pit – near Westhoughton. Five coal seams ran below the colliery. Just before 8am, at one of them – the Plodder Mine – there was an explosion loud enough to be heard three miles away. It was most likely caused by an accumulation of gas from a roof collapse a few days earlier. Before entering the mine, rescuers had to clear the shaft of one of the cages.

Some 545 miners were brought out from the neighbouring Arley and Trencherbone mines – some suffering burns, or ill-effects of the increasingly poor air. Most of them were able to go home after receiving initial medical treatment. But as each wave of survivors was brought out, their injuries were more severe. There was little hope for those who had been working close to the site of the explosion. Over the next several weeks, body after body was recovered from the mine. Some were burned beyond recognition while others betrayed little sign of trauma, as if the men had simply fallen into eternal sleep. It was later estimated that around 9 per cent of victims had died in the initial explosion, the remaining 91 per cent from gas poisoning. Local district nurses took care of the wounded and attended to the dead, placing personal belongings of the victims on top of coffins so that their families might more easily identify them.

Only four of those working at Plodder that day came back to the surface alive. One died shortly afterwards. Another the following day. One man was killed fighting a fire. William Davenport, a young fitter employed at the mine for around five years, had received severe burns and had not been expected to survive. But he returned to work in the mine. It is believed that he was protected by the explosion turning a tub on top of him which provided him with enough clean air to survive until he was rescued. His watch was ripped from his pocket, its workings broken; the timepiece stopped at just after 7.50am. It is now held in a local museum.

Forty-four bodies were brought out on Christmas Day alone. It was six weeks before the 344th body was recovered. One was never found. Twenty-four were initially unidentified.

Among the dead were men and boys ranging in age from teenagers, of whom thirty-five were aged 16 and under, to a man of 61. One victim, William Turton, was a father of eight. Thomas Molyneux was a 26-year-old married father of three. His youngest child was just 11 weeks old. Both Frederick Houghton and Anthony Doxey were killed on their first day in the mine.

Again, many families suffered multiple losses. Mrs Miriam Tyldesley lost her husband, four sons and two brothers, while Mrs John Baxter lost her husband and three sons.

As dangerous as their job was, miners were not the only workers faced with hazardous environments. Factories and mills up and down the country were occupied in what could be highly dangerous manufacturing activities. The Factory and Workshop Act 1901 brought in regulations to protect workers. Steam boilers, for example, had to be examined every fourteen months and be fitted with a safety valve, steam pressure gauge and water level gauge. The minimum working age for children was raised to twelve. Additional measures, like the Notice of Accidents Act 1906, helped to improve working conditions. In 1908 the first regulations relating to electrical safety were introduced. Although awareness of workplace safety was improving, legislation was still only basic and many companies had yet to implement new safety measures. One particular danger came from dust explosions.

In November 1911 there were two such tragedies. On 10th the Glasgow provender mill of William Primrose & Sons was the scene of an explosion thought to be caused by conditions within the mill. There was no system to collect dust, and large quantities accumulated on beams around the building. The lighting to the factory was by naked gas lights – one of which was on a long rubber hose that could be moved around the room. Somehow the gas ignited the flour dust, wrecking the building and causing five deaths and multiple injuries. Three of the dead were children playing in the street outside.

Just two weeks later, the huge premises of J. Bibby & Sons' Oil Cake Mills in Liverpool's docklands was the scene of an even greater explosion. The business occupied premises covering several acres of Great Howard Street, just a block away from the Mersey. It processed palm oil for animal feed. It was a modern facility with electric lighting and even a sprinkler system. But that did not prevent a disaster. On 24 November, shortly after the day shift had returned to work from the dinner break, there was a huge explosion in the basement when dust particles were ignited, either by a spark from the machinery, or perhaps from someone striking a match. The force of the explosion was so large that it blew the roof from the building and sprayed the surrounding area with debris. One young worker was killed when he was blown from the mill building and out on to the neighbouring railway line. Another young boy delivering bread in the street was killed when he was struck by a flying iron door.

Covered in dust and badly shaken, workers began to evacuate the building. They were followed by the walking wounded – many with burns and broken bones – who were helped to hospital only a short distance away. It was quickly overwhelmed with patients requiring emergency care. There were daring rescues of workers, who had taken refuge from a large fire inside, by clinging to window sills. According to Lord Derby, serving that year as Lord Mayor of Liverpool, in a telegram to the Home Secretary, as of that evening there had been 'thirteen deaths, and there are seventy-four injured persons who have been admitted to hospital, and are now as comfortable as can be expected. Many are sleeping under morphia.'

Local newspapers printed lists of those injured but able to go home, and those injured and remaining in hospital, many of whom would not survive. It was not until darkness had fallen that the search for those unable to escape the explosion and inferno could begin. The final death toll was thirty-nine, with more than a hundred seriously injured.

Britain's railways were frequently the scenes of accidents with multiple victims. Between October 1901 and June 1914 there were no less than thirty-four such incidents. In December 1901, the 5pm departure from Seaforth Sands caught fire as it entered the Dingle Tunnel. The fault stopped the train in the tunnel some eighty yards from the station. The driver tried to re-start the train but this resulted in 'arcing', which set fire to the wooden rear coach. A strong draught from a stiff breeze blowing into the tunnel fanned the flames and quickly all three carriages were alight. Twenty-nine passengers were evacuated and taken towards the station which was plunged into darkness when the electricity supply had to be cut. Lethal smoke began to fill the station and an attempt was made to evacuate it. The driver, guard, foreman and car cleaner, plus two passengers, unable to reach fresh air in time, all died.

In April the following year, a defective axle caused a morning commuter train to derail at Hackney Downs, resulting in it colliding with a bridge support. Three people were killed and 197 injured.

In July 1903 a special train, full of holidaymakers returning from the Isle of Man, arrived at the recently extended Glasgow St Enoch station. The inexperienced driver was unaware that the new platform to which he had been directed was 120 yards shorter than the others. He continued into the station at 20mph and, although he tried to brake as soon as he realised his mistake, hit the buffer stop, causing a violent crash. Thirteen people were killed instantly, three died later. Among the dead were four members of one family. Sixty-four people were injured.

Some accidents were caused, at least in part, by inclement conditions like the incident at Elliot Junction in Forfarshire on 28 December 1906, in which twenty-two people were killed when an express train crashed into the back of the train in front during a severe blizzard.

Or that in December 1904 in which four were killed when an express mail train, travelling through Aylesbury station at speed in the dark and fog clipped a platform on a curve and crashed into the station, breaking into pieces as it did. And another a few weeks later, at Cudworth, West Riding, in which three trains collided in the fog causing the deaths of seven people.

In July 1905, at Hall Road station, between Bootle and Formby stations, to the north of Liverpool, faulty points diverted the 4.30pm Liverpool Exchange to Southport express train into an empty local train which had been shunted into a siding. Both drivers were able to escape by jumping clear, but twenty people in the front coach of the express were killed and almost fifty others injured.

That September eleven were killed and seventy-one injured at Witham when all fourteen coaches of the London Liverpool Street to Cromer express derailed while going through the station. Several of the carriages were thrown on to the platform. Ten passengers were killed, as was a luggage porter, and seventy-one passengers injured.

On several occasions, drivers were accused of travelling at excessive speed resulting in serious accidents. On 1 July 1906, a boat train from Plymouth to London approached Salisbury at 70mph. The speed limit through the station was 20mph. The train was unable to negotiate a sharp bend at the eastern end of the station and derailed, crashing into a milk train and a light engine and killing twenty-eight people, including the driver. Following an investigation the speed limit was lowered to 15mph, and is still in effect today. Express trains were also required to stop at the station. Another speeding incident occurred at Shrewsbury in October 1907 when an overnight sleeper and mail train travelling from Manchester derailed on a sharp curve as it approached Shrewsbury station. Eighteen people were killed and thirty-three injured.

In September 1912, at Ditton Junction near Widnes, fifteen people were killed, including the driver and fireman, when the driver of the Chester to Liverpool express misread what was later declared to be confusing signalling, and travelled through a crossover with a speed limit of 15mph at an estimated 60mph. The locomotive derailed, turned on its side and struck the pier of an overbridge, breaking the engine in two. Six carriages crashed over the engine and formed a heap of wreckage. The impact had punctured gaslighting cylinders, which ignited to create an inferno.

The cause of the Ais Gill accident of September 1913 was attributed to a combination of underpowered engines, bad coal and human error. Two long passenger trains had left Carlisle bound for London St Pancras a few minutes apart. The trains both struggled to climb a steep gradient to the highest point on the Settle–Carlisle line. Both trains were run by the Midland Railway, whose smaller engines barely generated enough power to haul the heavy carriages. One driver had requested a pilot engine to assist him but was refused. Both engines had been filled with lower quality coal which was full of slack (a mixture of fine coal-gravel and dust) and very inefficient.

As it climbed, the first engine was forced to a stop half a mile from the summit, in order to build up enough steam to keep the brakes from automatically engaging. The driver and fireman told the guard they would be stationary for only a few minutes, so he did not lay detonators on the line, or walk down the line with his lantern to warn any following trains. Meanwhile, the second engine was now struggling. While the driver busied himself oiling the working parts of his engine, the fireman attended to a problem with an injector. The driver climbed back into the cab and both began to work on the injector. However, they were so distracted that they had missed the danger signal at the last signal box. They also missed the red lantern being frantically waved by the signalman. And they did not see the red lantern being held by the guard of the first train. By the time they looked up, the train in front was far too close to avoid. The second train crashed into the parcel van at the rear of the first train, demolishing it entirely, and smashing into the passenger carriage ahead. The roof of the parcels van slid over the second engine and sliced into the sleeper car behind it. Flammable gas began to escape from the cylinders for the gas-oil lighting system and ignited, quickly establishing a fire. Sixteen people in the first train were killed, while thirty-eight in the second were injured.

While mining disasters, mill explosions and rail crashes and the like are generally well remembered, and were sympathetically covered in the newspapers of the day, other terrible events were reported in sensationalist terms that make uncomfortable reading today – and then all-but forgotten by the generations that followed. One such event was the terrible fire that cost the lives of fifty-one or fifty-two (accounts vary) women in New Southgate, London.

The Colney Hatch Asylum was built in 1851 as the Second Middlesex County Asylum. It was designed to house more than 2,000 of London's 'pauper insane' and treated people with a range of conditions – a great many of whom had been diagnosed with epilepsy. Male and female patients were housed in separate wings.

London County Council took over the asylum in 1889. In 1896 a temporary extension to the building, containing five dormitories and made of Norwegian pine and corrugated iron, was opened to house 320 female patients in what was described as the 'Jewish Wing'. Immediately, the Lunacy Commission – the public body which oversaw asylums and the welfare of mentally ill patients in England and Wales – had warned that this would be a serious fire risk, but the extension went ahead. In the early hours of 27 January 1903, the Commission's assessment was proved correct. A fire, which started in a furnace room, was fanned by strong winds, and soon the entire extension was alight. Despite the brave efforts of the staff who, in all the chaos, attempted to rescue as many patients as possible, and the arrival of firefighters, that entire part of the building was lost. It was the worst peacetime fire in London's history since the medieval period – until the Grenfell fire of 2017. All of the dead were found either in their beds, huddled in corners, or in the long corridors.

There was limited newspaper coverage of the tragedy – certainly far less than would be devoted to the sinking of the *Titanic*, for example. And what coverage there was tended towards graphic descriptions of 'charred remains' and accusations of the panicking patients having made the situation worse. There were some sympathetic accounts of the patients' plight and the bravery of the nurses, but far more common were lurid headlines like 'Over Half a Hundred Lunatics Perish', and 'Patients who escaped uninjured are now roaming at large', as if the poor women were criminals to be feared, and as if this were as much a security emergency as it was a tragedy.

Commenting on the inquest into the Colney Hatch fire, *The Scotsman* described it as 'so great and deplorable a sacrifice of human life'.

Indeed, everyday life in the Edwardian era often proved perilous.

CHAPTER 9

Upstairs, Downstairs – The Edwardians at Home

> The Ideal Home Exhibition ... is being planned on a colossal scale ... Construction, decoration, lighting and heating, ventilation, furniture, recreation, hygiene and cleaning, food, cookery and the garden ... So much depends on the home life that it is strange an exhibition of this kind has never been held before.
>
> *Daily News*, March 1908

Contemporary popular culture tells us that the Edwardian age was a time of plenty. Of over-indulgence. Of richly decorated, well-lit, warm homes. Of luxury and of leisure. For some, this is true. If you were a member of the upper and upper-middle classes, then life could be very comfortable indeed.

But of 40 million or so Britons, only 3 per cent fell into those categories. For everyone else, life was challenging.

Increasing homelessness had become a major problem and, while the poverty-stricken of a specific area had the local workhouse to go to, those who had no fixed address had to rely on 'casual wards' established in many parishes to provide basic food and accommodation for one night only. No matter how needy, their next night had to be spent in a different casual ward.

In 1906 the government's Vagrancy Committee Report called the homeless a 'vagrant army'. It recommended: 'Tickets be issued by the police to persons who are in search of work, the ticket to be for a definite route and available only for a month, the police having power to alter the route if satisfied that such a course is necessary.'

The plan was to allow the ticket holder to leave the casual ward early in the morning with their midday meal of bread and cheese and to travel to the next casual ward where there would be an informal labour bureau with details of work available locally. The report also suggested that, instead of the existing sentence of fourteen days in prison, convicted vagrants be sentenced to just one day's imprisonment. Each conviction would be recorded, and 'habitual vagrants' – those convicted more than three times – could be sent to labour colonies for periods ranging from six months to two years.

In 1910 it was reported that 'homelessness in London is becoming an issue'. Each night the Salvation Army were feeding and sheltering upwards of 640 homeless people gathering on the Embankment.

In 1909, Maud Pember Reeves gathered a team of visitors from the Fabian Women's Group's Motherhood Special Fund Committee to look into family life for the working classes living in London's Lambeth. Over a period of four years they would make weekly visits to the families of thirty-six mothers of infants. Twice a month the families were visited and examined by Dr Ethel Bentham. Records were kept of household expenditure and verbatim accounts of the interviews were recorded.

In 1913 all of the information was published in the report 'Round About A Pound A Week'. The report found that Lambeth, like other working-class areas of Britain, had a far higher rate of infant mortality than wealthier parts. It declared that, had those children been 'well housed, well fed, well clothed and well-tended from birth', then the outcomes would have undoubtedly been very different. The report made several recommendations including that the state should pay family endowments, train midwives, cover the cost of burials, provide free school meals, introduce a minimum wage and provide clean, spacious and airy affordable housing for poorer families.

Nutrition was particularly problematic. Most working-class families relied upon bread as the basis of its diet. Cheap, reliable and filling, bread was something that was always attainable and rarely changed in quality, no matter how financially flush a family might be that week. The Lambeth families generally enjoyed a roast dinner on Sunday, with cold cuts and leftovers making up several of the meals for the remainder of the week. Potatoes, too, were almost ever-present, but fresh milk was something that household budgeting could not always provide. Two years earlier, for example, a long, dangerous heatwave and drought, which destroyed much of the nation's grazing, led to poor milk production and a steep rise in milk prices.

Although it was recognised that fresh milk was the preferred follow-on and supplemental food for infants after breast milk, few families could afford it in the quantities required. Through no fault of their parents, as the report made clear, most infants were swiftly moved on to sharing the rest of the family's normal food.

The Fabian report cited many examples that give an insight into working class life:

> 'Mr W', for example was a toy-packer, earning 20s per week. While his wife was once a machinist who had earned 10s per week, she was now out of work and concentrating on keeping house and awaiting the arrival of their baby. She is clean and thrifty, writes a good hand, and keeps excellent accounts. She is nineteen. Out of the 2s retained by the husband, he pays 6d a week into a clothing club, and of course his 4d is deducted for State Insurance. With the rest 'he does what he likes'. Sometimes he likes to give his wife an extra penny for her housekeeping.

'Mrs W' was typical of married working-class women. While the women's lives before marriage had been hard, they had at least had the benefit of interactions with their peers and some financial independence:

> It is obvious that with these young men marriage is, so far, both pleasant and successful; the young women's lives are far more changed. They tell you that they are a bit lonely at times, and miss the companionship of the factory life and the money of their own to spend.

Even for the four million or so of the newly expanding lower-middle classes there was no featherbed. There was, however, room for aspiration and life showed signs of improvement. New employment opportunities in offices, in retail and in service industries ensured a class of Britons who had steady well-paid year-round work. This emerging group was seen as a significant new market. Two newspapers – the *Daily Mail* (1896) and the *Daily Mirror* (1903) – were established by brothers Alfred and Harold Harmsworth (ennobled as Viscounts Northcliffe and Rothermere, respectively) to serve the new audience.

The new classes also needed houses. More than one million new homes were built during the Edwardian period. Some 800,000 of these were in terraces either of small houses, palisades or townhouses. Some 400,000 flats were constructed, as buildings were forced upwards rather than outwards. On the edge of towns, in the new suburbs, there was more space and some 250,000 semi-detached, and 180,000 detached homes were built, as well as 100,000 of the new bungalows – the first of which had been built at Westgate-on-Sea between 1869 and 1870. The term 'bungalow' came from Hindi, and meant simply 'house in the Bengal style'. The new homes were not a deliberate copy, but when a journalist noted that they reminded him of the homes he had seen in India, the name stuck. Bungalows became highly popular with the middle classes, as did life in the new suburbs.

Improvements and expansions in public transport enabled population centres to grow outwards. Many of those who had a choice now elected to move to the edge of town, away from industrial areas and to where the air was fresher and there was more space.

And where there was more space, there was an opportunity to try out new architectural styles – many of them inspired by the past. So-called 'cottage style' architecture was the most popular and lent itself well to the popular Arts and Crafts movement. Wider plots allowed for sweeping roofs, deep, low gables and an altogether prettier aspect. And from 1910 fashion moved towards a neo-Georgian, more symmetrical, style – although the outbreak of war meant that there were far fewer properties of that style built.

Nowhere was more attention paid to providing an attractive environment in which to live than in the new purpose-built garden suburbs. A Garden City Movement had been proposed by urban planner Sir Ebenezer Howard OBE in 1898 in his book *To-Morrow: A Peaceful Path to Real Reform*, which described utopian settlements where humans lived surrounded by nature. Places where satellite settlements were divided proportionally into areas of residence, industry and agriculture, and were separated from their cities by beautiful greenbelts. The first to be inspired by the idea was Letchworth Garden City in Hertfordshire, on which work began in 1903. There was so much public interest that the Great Northern Railway ran day excursions, for 3s 3d, to see the new settlement.

Around the same time there were variations on the movement in which primarily residential suburbs were established. The first of these was Hampstead Garden Suburb, which was actually north of Hampstead, west of Highgate and east of Golders Green, on land purchased from Eton College by Dame Henrietta Barnett. The suburb was not designed to be self-contained and rules for its construction were set out in the Hampstead Garden Suburb Act of 1906. By 1909 – just eighteen months after work had begun – some 2,000 people lived in the suburb.

The *Hampstead News* described the latest developments in July that year: 'In about two months' time sixty-one ladies earning their own living will be housed in a Baillie Scott quadrangle, each in her own self-contained flat, and her main meals ready cooked for her on her return from her day's work.'

The quadrangle became known as Waterlow Court and consisted of fifty-three, three-to-five-room flats and a communal dining area. It was deemed ideal for the new single working women, not wealthy enough to employ servants of their own, but in need of some domestic assistance. A communal kitchen, a small common room and quarters for the housekeepers and porters rounded out the complex, while the grounds featured a bicycle shed and allotment strips where the women could grow their own flowers. Residents of the suburb could already avail themselves of many societies and clubs.

Dame Henrietta wanted the scheme to cater for all classes of people and all income groups. It is true that there were a wide variety of employment represented – although by far the largest was those working as staff or servants for homeowners. But there were also jewellers, surveyors, doctors, dentists, an actress, an author, several teachers and a barrister. But there were artisans too – such as house painters, plumbers and carpenters. In 1911, at 2 Temple Grove – a charming, white-painted cottage style property – lived Charles Luck and his wife Mary Ann. Charles was a 51-year-old carver and gilder. The couple had six children, three of whom were at school, and the other three worked as a 'warehousewoman', 'sewing machinist', and 'dress maker'. One of their next-door-neighbours worked as a joiner and the other a journalist. This pattern of office workers living next door to managers and secretaries, living next door to embroiderers and artists, living next door to law clerks and civil servants, repeated itself throughout the growing suburb.

And there were a fair number of architects in residence – more than a dozen of them in 1911. As at Letchworth, the then Buxton-based architectural partnership of Barry Parker and Raymond Unwin were brought in to oversee the design, while a number of other established and up-and-coming architects assisted with individual house design. Not everyone was entirely enamoured with the new architecture. 'B.A.', writing in *John Bull*, noted:

> Some of the houses are indeed funny ... the structure of the houses seems sound, but they ought not to have cost much to build ... the fittings of the house are of the ordinary kind ... the stucco elevations are cheap, and the houses, although they cover a lot of ground, are not carried high ... if the present freakish and quixotic methods are pursued, the tenants will not possess a valuable and eligible property in the future.

While the housing stock was varied, the use of similar building materials – red, purple and brown bricks, roughcast in its natural tone, or painted white or cream with red tiled roofs – and elements – large, elaborate chimneys, dormer or bay windows – all helped to create an attractive palette and a cohesive, harmonious feel. The careful and generous planting of hedges, bushes, trees and plants made it the quintessential leafy suburb.

Dame Henrietta wanted roads to be wider than was normal with at least 50ft between houses on opposite sides of any road, with a much lower than usual housing density of no more than eight houses per acre. Houses were to be separated by hedges rather than walls. It was quiet, too – with no church bells to disturb residents. And all woods and public gardens were free for all to enter.

For centuries, road surfaces across Britain had been notoriously uneven and prone to breaking up and rutting. Even the new 'macadam' road surfaces, made from stones and sand and invented by John Loudon McAdam became fragile and dusty under heavy use. Various attempts had been made to stabilise the surface by binding it with a viscous substance. In 1834 John Henry Cassell patented his 'lava stone', which worked by sandwiching the macadam between layers of tar and sand.

However, with the increasing popularity of motorised vehicles, improvements in road construction were urgently needed. In 1901 Edgar Purnell Hooley, the Welsh-born Nottinghamshire county surveyor, was walking in the Derbyshire village of Denby. He noticed a patch of road that was unusually smooth. He was told that a barrel of tar had spilled on to the road and that slag from the local furnaces had been poured over it to clean it up. The emergency patch-up had unintentionally invented a strong, solid, smooth road surface with no dust and no rutting. The following year Hooley patented a similar process which mixed tar and aggregate and compacted it using a steam roller. In 1903 he formed the Tar Macadam Syndicate Ltd and registered 'Tarmac' as a trademark.

If the invention of the internal combustion engine and improved road surfaces had made it easier for people to live further from the centre of town, then it was the introduction of electricity to domestic properties that surely brought about the biggest change to daily lives in Britain.

The first public electricity generator in Britain had been installed in 1881 in Godalming. The following year the government had passed the Electric Light Act which regulated the early industry and enabled the Board of Trade to authorise a local authority, company or person to provide electricity. By 1915 there would be 600 separate electricity supply companies. To this end, over the next few years, various power stations were built across the country – in Liverpool, Belfast and Bristol for example. And within London itself – at Deptford and Holburn Viaduct. Council built and owned power stations would be linked together creating what would eventually become the National Grid.

On a domestic level, however, the introduction of electricity to private houses was slow. Inevitably it was the homes of richer citizens which were the first to install the new magical system. In general, electric lighting came first. Often only one light in one room, usually the kitchen – where good clear lighting was of more importance.

But some early incarnations of electrical appliances were too big for powering in that way. In 1901 Hubert Cecil Booth, a man previously famed for the design of, among other things, Ferris wheels, invented the first electrically powered vacuum cleaner. It was so large that the vacuum pump and engine were horse-drawn. A long pipe was fed into the house to do the cleaning. When a householder used the service, fascinated crowds would gather in the street to watch the machine in action. Within the decade, however, a more recognisable upright domestic home vacuum cleaner was available to buy.

There was no standardisation in electricity supply from one area to another but, in 1904, US inventor Harvey Hubbell created an adapter plug that enabled non-lightbulb devices to be connected to the supply via the light socket. As the number of household electrical gadgets coming on to the British market increased, so did the number of wires trailing down from a central light to various parts of a room.

Although Britain's electricity supply is now regarded as one of the world's safest – particularly when it comes to wall sockets – in the early days, using electricity in British homes was not without risks. Few homeowners understood how it even worked. And while there were basic regulations, these were largely ignored. Britain's early electricity was not earthed – regulations requiring that would not come into law until the mid-1930s. In 1911 the first three-pronged plug with an earth connection was brought to Britain by the AP Lundberg company. There was also little insulation which, when it was present, was usually made from dangerously flammable substances like cotton or paper. Overloading was a common cause of fires. As were sparks which, in homes which still ran most of the lighting with gas, was a terrible hazard.

The first permanent telephone link in Europe had been installed by Alexander Graham Bell in Plymouth in 1877. The following year he had demonstrated his system to Queen Victoria who had it installed at Osborne House with lines to Cowes, Southampton and London. The same year, Bell had registered his telephone company in Britain and opened three telephone exchanges in London, and others in Glasgow, Manchester, Liverpool, Sheffield, Edinburgh, Birmingham and Bristol.

Bell's main rival was The Edison Telephone Company of London Ltd, which opened a further three exchanges in the capital. In 1901 the first municipal telephone exchanges were opened in Glasgow, Tunbridge Wells, Brighton and Portsmouth.

The General Post Office (GPO), which had controlled the nation's telegraph lines since 1870, established its own London exchange in 1902, which was quickly followed by more across the capital. The company also introduced a cut-price call charge between the hours of 8pm and 6am. While only the wealthiest installed home telephones to begin with, anyone with a few pence to spare and someone to reach on the other end of the line, could use them. Public telephone calling offices were established in towns and cities across the nation and were, theoretically, available to all.

In 1912 the GPO took over the National Telephone Company's system to become the monopoly telephone service provider across Britain – with the exception of municipal services in Hull, Portsmouth and Guernsey. The GPO telephone systems now ran 1,500,000 miles of wire between 1,565 exchanges, and employed 9,000 workers serving 561,738 subscribers. Telephone lines became ubiquitous enough that they were sometimes targeted by suffragist campaigners.

Since the telephone lines were connected to electricity, there were inevitable accidents, although British newspapers certainly reported more telephone electrocution incidents in America than in Britain. Closer to home, at least according to doctors, the danger of the telephone came from its capacity to spread disease – particularly those telephones that were in public calling offices. A number of newspapers reported that an article had been published in *The Lancet* warning that telephone mouthpieces harboured all manner of germs. In response, the government, via the Postmaster General, announced that a telephone cleansing programme was under way, and that a new method of disinfecting was to be implemented in future. The *Nottingham Journal* remained unconvinced and rather mocked the very idea that the:

> death dealing germ is a dreadful bogey ... our grandfathers had a knack of living to seventy or upwards with a careless disregard of possible microbes, and the present generation would do well to take a leaf out of their book. We are getting supersensitive and timorous in these matters, and life will not be worth living if we are going to allow ourselves to be scared by a too credulous fear of the germ.

Edwardian 'snowflakes' aside, the British public were becoming more aware of issues of health and lifestyle – an understanding of the roles of what Polish-American biochemist Casimir Funk would, in 1911, name 'vitamines' was increasing. This was thanks in no small part to the low-priced weekly magazines that had become increasingly popular since the turn of the century. Titles such as *Home Notes*, *Home Chat* and *Home Companion* featured regular articles on nutrition and childcare in particular, alongside their main content on the latest fashions in homestyle and lifestyle.

Following the lead of their monarch, wealthier Edwardians aspired to all things French. This was particularly true when it came to cuisine. The rich entertained one another with lavish multi-coursed dinner parties but increasingly took pleasure in dining out – at fashionable and glamorous restaurants, which were becoming so popular among the monied classes that hotels like Claridge's, The Ritz and The Savoy remodelled their dining rooms into chic restaurants.

The period also saw the rise of Auguste Escoffier who was, if not precisely a 'celebrity' chef, certainly a celebrated one. Born in Provence, Escoffier's partnership with hotelier Cesar Ritz brought him to prominence. He brought in a workforce of experienced French chefs, reorganised kitchen practices, and formalised classic French recipes. Even a dismissal from The Savoy in 1898, for 'gross negligence and breaches of duty and mismanagement' had done little to tarnish his legacy. But the Frenchman did have a rival – in the form of the Cockney former scullery maid, Rosa Lewis, who ran the Cavendish Hotel on Mayfair's Jermyn Street – her original premises were demolished in 1964 to make way for the current hotel. Using her hard work, endearing wit and fine culinary skills, Lewis had worked her way up from scrubbing the floors at the age of 12, to cook by the age of 16. By 1900 she had run the kitchens of high society figures, prepared feasts for aristocracy and royalty and, in 1902, made sufficient profit from the suppers she had prepared for twenty-nine large events celebrating the coronation, to purchase the Cavendish Hotel. It featured a private dining room in which the aristocracy could entertain guests out of public sight. This assurance of discretion, along with her extraordinary food, kept guests coming, with some using the Cavendish as their regular London abode. Rosa Lewis's career was dramatised in the 1970s television drama *The Duchess of Duke Street*.

For those from the middle or working classes, options for eating something cooked outside of the home were rather limited. Lyons had opened its first tea shop in Piccadilly in 1894. From 1909 it opened the first of its famous Corner House tea shops and cafes. They were, effectively, the first large restaurant chain that catered specifically for the middle and working classes.

The majority of the population, though, did not have money to spend on extravagant afternoon teas or picnics. Most meals, of course, were taken at home. Across London, particularly in the East End, the pie and mash shop predominated. But across the country it was the fish and chip shop that reigned supreme. It is not at all clear who 'invented' fish and chips, but it began to appear around 1860. Fried fish was probably first introduced by Jews in London's East End. Chips first became popular in the northern counties of Yorkshire and Lancashire. Both Bow in London, and Mossley near Oldham, are among those places laying claims to be the first to combine the two. Most likely, as with most popular food combinations, the partnering was a gradual inevitability, rather than a eureka moment, or accidental revelation. The great developments in trawler fishing, combined with Britain's extensive railway network meant plentiful fish in most parts of the country and led to the establishment of thousands of shops serving the dish. By 1910 there were more than 25,000 fish and chip shops operating in Britain, and in 1913 the National Federation of Fish Friers was established.

For many Edwardians, fish and chips were hugely popular and formed an important component of the weekly food for the average family. So popular was fish and chips as a meal that countless local newspaper advertisements referred to them – not only to the shops themselves, but advertisements for 'up-to-date chipped potato and fried fish apparatus', like that of Richard Kirk, tinner and brazier of Chesterfield, as well as for existing businesses that came up for sale.

In 1903 the quintessentially British cup of tea began to taste more like the cuppa we recognise today when John Sumner Jr, the son and grandson of Birmingham pharmacist-grocers, decided to create a new tea he could sell in his shop. What he hit upon proved a true innovation and made great use of what had previously been a waste product from fancy tea production. The edges of tea leaves were generally discarded and used for only poor-quality teas. However, tea made from these 'fannings' was generally fuller flavoured and stronger, and considered to have a greater calming effect than the larger, broken pieces of leaves. And it was the so-called 'dust' from Ceylon tea that Sumner chose to make his new blend. Of course, in a stroke of marketing genius, he did not call it 'dust tea', but chose to name the offcuts 'tips', and gave his new brand the rather mystical sounding name of 'Ty Phoo', which was inspired by a Mandarin Chinese word for 'doctor'. Thus, Ty Phoo Tipps tea was born, although the additional 'p' was initially due to a printing error. With the assumed association of the tea being good for one's health and digestion, Sumner's assertion that the tips were the tastiest part of the leaf, and the fact that a smaller amount of tea produced a reliable strong drink, Typhoo Tipps soon became a popular British brand.

Another beverage, but one which did not find its way on to every dining table, was Perrier water. It is another of those favourites of the middle-class for which we have to thank the Harmsworth family – this time St John, the younger brother of Lords Northcliffe and Rothermere. With the family keen to establish business relationships with France, St John was sent to the Continent to learn the language. He found himself in Nimes and bought into a small spa there – previously owned by a Dr Louis Perrier. St John closed the spa, but maintained use of the spring there, renaming it 'Source Perrier'. He had the water bottled into specially designed green glass bottles in the shape of Indian exercise clubs, exported it to Britain and began to sell it as a healthy alternative to local water supplies. However, thanks to improvements in the sewage system and water treatment, most towns and cities now had safe tap water. Making the new product a success would take some careful and canny marketing. Harmsworth invested heavily in advertising. These emphasised Perrier's French origin and suggested that drinking it with meals aided digestion. It was, thanks to its natural sparkle, 'the Champagne of mineral waters'. And its regular presence on the pages of the *Daily Mail* made it seem as if it were ubiquitous. Advertisements asserted that it was 'on the menu of every prominent banquet'. To reinforce its association with a healthy lifestyle, various sporting icons of the day were paid for their endorsement. Before long it became de rigueur at golf club bars, and hotels with 95 per cent of sales being at British and US outlets. In 1908, during the Franco-British Exhibition to mark the Entente Cordiale, Perrier hosted its own pavilion.

For most households, though, ordinary tap water was sufficient. This did not mean the average family could not take advantage of the seemingly constant innovations in food processing, especially when it came to home cooking. The British housewife, and housekeeper or cook, had an increasing range of pre-packaged goods from which to choose.

Marmite first came on to the market in 1902. In the late nineteenth century German scientist Justus Liebig had discovered, by chance, that the leftover brewer's yeast – essential to the making of beer – could be made into a strong flavoured, umami-tasting concentrate that could be used as a spread, or in cooking. The Marmite Food Company was established in the brewing town of Burton upon Trent, where there was a plentiful supply of the required raw ingredients. The product took its name from a French casserole dish and was initially sold in earthenware pots of a similar shape. Although not to everyone's taste, Marmite proved a versatile foodstuff in its own right and as an ingredient.

Liebig made another important contribution to the British dinner table. He had already developed the process for making a stable and easy to work with beef extract. It was known as 'Lemco' – from his company name of Liebig's Extract of Meat Company'. In 1899 he began to market a cheaper version for household use – it was named Oxo. In 1910 the first Oxo cubes came on to the market.

The British love of brown sauce also dates from this time. Frederick Gibson Garton was a Nottinghamshire grocer who had a penchant for invention. He created his own sauces and relishes in a small factory at the back of his New Basford home. His popular brown sauce owed a lot to the influences of India, and made good use of ingredients from the British Empire – tamarind, mace, cloves, ginger and cayenne pepper among them. There are several versions of how the name so familiar to generations came about, including one that claims Garton heard that a restaurant in the Houses of Parliament was serving his sauce which had apparently become a favourite with politicians. And because he recognised a good marketing strategy when he saw it, he registered the name 'HP Sauce'. Whatever the truth, to this day the bottles still carry a picture of the Houses of Parliament.

In debt to the Midland Vinegar Company of Birmingham, Garton was forced to hand over the rights and recipe to the sauce, and several others. In 1904 Daddies Sauce came on to the market as a cheaper product than HP, but with roughly the same ingredients.

A raft of other familiar sauces began to grace the dining tables of British homes. Henderson's Relish was the creation of Sheffield grocer Henry Henderson. Similar to the popular Worcestershire Sauce, the relish was produced without anchovies and so would later prove popular as a vegetarian-friendly alternative. The first commercial salad cream was introduced into the UK in 1914 by Heinz. In 1905, Cadbury introduced its Dairy Milk chocolate, which within a decade became their best-selling product. Rival brand Fry's introduced its Turkish Delight bar in 1914.

In 1908 Lord Northcliffe – as ever the middle-class housewife's best friend – opened the first Daily Mail Ideal Home Exhibition at Olympia. He had intended it to be a marketing tool for the newspaper, but the event was to become an established British institution in its own right. In 1908, 90 per cent of the population rented their home, but this did not mean that they were without aspiration. The middle-classes in particular were beginning to find that after the essentials of rent, food and heating were budgeted in they had a little disposable income, and the exhibition offered plenty of options for what to spend that on. The scale of that first exhibition was impressive and took more than 3,000 workers one week to build. Visitors, who paid one shilling, came in droves, and were told by publicity material to expect to see the 'streets of a town lined with hundreds of bright little buildings of varying shape and design – red roofed cottages, brown bungalows, and gaily coloured pavilions'. Instead of traditional stands, all the very latest products and gadgets were displayed in 'rooms'. There were queues to tour a landscaped garden and to see the various furnished homes.

The exhibition helped to stimulate debate about better housing conditions for Edwardian Britain as well as drawing attention to the new possibilities of what home life might be in the future.

CHAPTER 10

The Gentle Art of Beauty, the Conceits of Fashion

> The doors of this immense New Building will be opened wide to all the world ... no cards are required for admission, and everyone will be welcome.
>
> Selfridges pre-opening advertisement,
> *Evening Standard*, 11 March 1909

When it came to the Edwardian ideal of beauty, no more perfect example could be found than Lily Elsie. Throughout the Edwardian era she was one of the most photographed women in the country. With her large blue eyes, charming profile, and lustrous hair, she precisely fitted the fair-skinned, dark-haired and wide-eyed Edwardian natural beauty ideal. Fair skin, untanned and free of freckles, was indicative of someone of higher class and so not required to spend much time out of doors.

Of particular importance, Lily Elsie possessed the kind of luminous beauty that photographs captured so well. She was a talented stage actress and classical singer, the star of Franz Lehar's operetta *The Merry Widow*, and her frequent appearances on the London stage, made her one of the most famous performers of her time. Elsie and other famous actresses, like Gladys Cooper and Maude Fealy, became beauty icons.

The Edwardian beauty industry, although not invisible, was not something which bombarded everyday life. Indeed, advertising and marketing in general was a far subtler affair. For those who wished to find it, however, beauty advice and beauty products had been widely available for some years. Particularly when it came to the pages of magazines and journals.

Women's magazines, of which there were several by 1900, regularly featured advice on skincare, haircare, and gentle enhancement of the appearance. In 1861 Samuel Orchart Beeton (the husband of famous domestic writer Isabel 'Mrs' Beeton) founded a fashion and culture newspaper for upper-class women which would eventually morph into what we know today as *Harper's Bazaar*.

In 1901 it was known as *The Queen, the Lady's Newspaper and Court Chronicle* and featured many advertisements for popular fashionable beauty treatments. Like that for 'Circassian Toiletine', suitable for 'all who are troubled with blemishes, redness, or roughness of the skin on the face or hands ... after a few applications it will make the face perfectly smooth, and at the same time impart to it a beautiful healthy tone'.

Calvert's Carbolic Toilet Soap 'for the skin and complexion', was antiseptic and emollient. Despite modern perceptions of its utilitarian nature and distinctive scent, carbolic soap was a useful and effective product. It killed bacteria, was mildly deodorising and helped to clear up acne. Its popularity has waned over the years, but it is still distributed by the Red Cross to disaster victims to ensure basic hygiene.

'Vinolia' cream was 'a plastic emollient cream' for 'itching, face spots and all skin irritation', including chilblains. It was also considered healing for eczema. The Vinolia company had been producing various skincare products for several decades and its soap would be used aboard the RMS *Titanic*.

James's advertised its depilatory as 'Hair Destroyer'. Conversely, it also produced a Herbal Pomade which promised 'long flowing eyelashes' and the production of whiskers, beard and moustaches which, for the more mature gentleman at least, was a vital element of Edwardian personal style. It was also claimed to 'cause hair to grow on bald places or scanty partings like magic'. James's products could be purchased from chemists, which certainly imparted a degree of confidence in their efficacy. They were also available from a residential premises at

268 Caledonian Road, Islington – just half a mile down the road from Pentonville prison.

A particularly popular James's product was their 'Herbal Ointment', reassuringly 'made from herbs only', which would instantly 'remove "Pimples, Black Specks and Unsightly Blotches"' on the face, neck, arms, and hands. The seemingly miraculous ointment also promised to 'entirely eradicate freckles, sunburn and roughness occasioned by the winds ... and prevents the approach of wrinkles'. While the usual emollients would undoubtedly work to ease the latter three issues, they would not remove freckles.

There was no law requiring ingredients of such concoctions to be listed, but manufacturers were conscious that the British public were becoming more cautious and so advertising often declared the 'natural' character of the products.

However, users had only the manufacturers' words that their products contained nothing harmful. Quite often, of course, they did. And 'natural' and 'herbal' did not necessarily mean either efficacious or safe. Early face preparations, particularly those intended to lighten the skin – or at least to make it appear lighter – were notorious for containing lead and arsenic. Products for dealing with freckles usually contained at least a small quantity of an acid or a bleach and could barely be considered 'safe'. The problem was that, like many of their ancestors, Edwardians generally considered freckles blemishes to be hidden, or preferably eradicated. Whereas the modern perception is that freckles can be youthful, natural and flattering, Edwardians associated them with the labouring classes. Worse still, with upper-class lifestyles bringing them more fresh air and sunlight, freckles were springing up and 'spoiling' the skin of the wealthy and refined.

Eradicating freckles became something of a national obsession, and this brought a plethora of freckle removers to the market. For those seeking beauty advice, but unable to afford high-end beauty salons, monthly journals like *The Gentlewoman* came to the rescue. Its 'Gentle Art of Beauty' page of December 1902 offered 'answers to questions on all subjects relating to the Toilet, but not on matters of Health and Disease (which the editor regards as too serious and delicate an undertaking to be dealt with in a newspaper)'. Written by 'Venus', bespoke advice on 'colours, styles, modes of arranging the hair etc' would be given to correspondents providing a photograph and description of their colouring and height. Various answers were published with the nom-de-plume, in brackets, of each correspondent – after all, when it came to matters of beauty and personal care, anonymity was everything. 'Shrimp' was advised to use Icilma Castile Soap twice a week, 'Red Nose' was directed to 'rub in a little of Clark's Glycola' to treat their rough, red skin. A 'little adherent cream-toned face powder' should then be applied and alternatively – and less helpfully – she was advised to 'wear a veil'.

The *Weekly Journal*, which described itself as the 'Largest Halfpenny Paper in the British Empire' was aimed at 'men, women and children' and offered advice that was rather more accessible to the average Briton.

Although the 'Simple Hair Tonic' made from soaking 'a penny-worth of quassia chips' in boiling water, steeping for an hour, and straining before brushing through the hair at night – 'exceptionally good for children's hair', possibly had more to do with its anti-parasitic properties and suitability as a head lice treatment than any shine-enhancing qualities. Practical considerations, of course, came first. And it was undoubtedly gentler than the solution for greasy hair, which involved adding saltpetre and ammonia to a soapy mixture and using it in 'a small quantity (according to judgement) for washing the hair'.

Some Edwardian beauty advice may prove familiar with those keen on modern selfcare practices. Women were advised to apply castor or coconut oil nightly to lashes to condition them – and to leave substantial tidying of the brows to professional experts.

For those who did prefer to avail themselves of some professional expertise before treating their skin, countless salons were operating. Advertisements for such salons, and their more expensive, exclusive products generally appeared in journals such as *The Gentlewoman*, amid those for various continental European finishing schools. It was generally assumed that the more salubrious the address, the higher up the social scale the clientele and the more effective, or at least expensive, the treatments would be. Anyone attending the premises of Eleanor Adair on Bond Street expected the crème-de-la-crème of treatments.

Eleanor Adair was really Mrs Eleanor Huntley Nicholson, née Hanley. Born in Liverpool in 1864, she was the wife of a Lieutenant-Colonel in the Royal Army Medical Corps. It was not unusual for such businesses to use assumed names. The beauty industry was still regarded with a degree of suspicion, and not a little distaste, and a number of proprietors preferred an element of anonymity. The founder of Cyclax in South Molton Street, Fanny Forsythe, began her business under the assumed name of 'Mrs Hemming'.

Eleanor Adair opened in 1900 and would remain in business for thirty years. Eleanor was one of the foremost beauty experts of her era. Her wide range of products were sold from her three salons (she opened one in Paris in 1902 and another in New York in 1903) by mail order, and from chemists in places as stylish and far distant as Monte Carlo, Geneva, Algiers and Rio de Janeiro.

With her first husband, from whom she divorced in 1903, she had spent several years in India, and she used that history to market her products. There was considerable intrigue into any exotic secret that might be discovered in far-off lands. In 1905 the *Daily Mirror* published 'some secret methods learned in the East'.

Adair, too, would write about her 'secrets' and 'discoveries' in the 'Vale of Kashmir' or the 'Temple of Ganesh'. Beauty experts of the time believed that wrinkles and other signs of ageing in the skin had several causes, some of which we would recognise today – loss of elasticity, slow circulation, poor diet, and weakened facial muscles from 'overuse', worry and illness. This could be treated using a combination of facial exercises, massage and the application of a 'muscle oil' which would help to build up the flesh so that the skin on top appeared smooth and wrinkle-free. Adair's Ganesh Eastern Muscle Oil was, perhaps, her most popular product. The precise ingredients were a closely guarded secret, but recipes of the time for similar products to be made at home included some sort of vegetable oil – usually sweet almond or olive, mixed with resins and aromatic essential oils like wintergreen, camphor and rose.

Adair's advertisements declared her muscle oil 'The Great Beautifier', and those with 'fine lines or heavy wrinkles or hollows …

skin tinged with sallowness and discoloration' to begin using the product 'immediately under Mrs Adair's personal directions'.

In 1901 advertisements quoted one Mrs Deborah Primrose as saying, 'Mrs Adair's Eastern Muscle-Developing Oil fills up hollows, makes the skin smooth and white, removes all sorts of lines, no matter how long-standing, and her Skin Tonic reduces puffiness under the eyes.' Later titled Dame Deborah Primrose, the critic was a well-known writer for a women's magazine.

The Adair system did popularise some skin treatments still in use today. In 1903 an advertorial advised a method for facial massage that could be done at home and involved gently tapping and face with the weaker fingers. The range would eventually extend to include treatments and preparations for acne, those pesky freckles and brown spots, as well as beauty sachets instead of soap to cleanse the face, a 'soothing and cleansing lotion for day use', and Spagnette Cream 'Extracted from the Irish Bog Peat, gives an attractive freshness to the skin'. For those unable to attend in person a printed guide containing her 'New Lecture on Beauty Culture. with sketches and direction for home treatment' could be mail-ordered for 1s 1d.

Adair salons also offered sophisticated electrolysis treatments and even these, with the appropriate machine, were suitable for at-home treatment. One advertisement of 1906 pictured Eleanor Adair dressed in a sari and using her 'Adair Electro-Coil Battery'. In 1902 she was granted patents for two 'strap' products – one for forehead, one for chin – which claimed to use electricity to tone flabby chins and smooth furrowed brows. The product line expanded quickly and there was soon a Ganesh Nasal Clamp which purported to 'cure wide nostrils, giving a perfectly shaped nose.' One of the beauty experts who trained at her New York salon was Florence Graham, later known as Elizabeth Arden.

In 1906 Helena Rubinstein placed a full-page advertorial in *The Queen* espousing her Maison de Beaute Valaze in London's Grafton Street, the products she sold and treatments she performed, which were based on what she called the 'Viennese School' – Rubinstein had grown up in Krakow, which at the time was part of Austria-Hungary, before emigrating to Australia where she established her first salon. Arriving in London, she shrewdly saw the potential of tapping into a burgeoning new market, and was one of the first purveyors of beauty to divide skin into types, and prescribe different skincare regimes. She was also one of the first entrepreneurs to really see the potential of mass marketing. Her Crème Valaze was the first skincare product specifically for moisturising. It came complete with its own origin story which may, or may not, have been true – details were certainly developed over the several decades that it formed part of Rubinstein's range. And it was a great success.

By now, more of the brand names we know today were appearing on high streets. Pears Soap had been trading since 1807. Vaseline also dated back many decades. Yardley had been producing soap since at least 1770, and by 1910 had opened premises in Bond Street and introduced a popular shaving soap, reckoned to be the superior of anything made on the Continent. A decades-old American business, The Pond's Extract Company had set up in the UK in 1878. It introduced its Vanishing Cream to the British market in 1905, and its Cold Cream the following year. At the more exclusive end of the market familiar names included Penhaligon, established in the late 1860s by Cornish barber William Penhaligon. He moved to London, establishing shops in Jermyn Street and St James' Street. In 1903 Penhaligon's was granted its first royal warrant by Queen Alexandra.

Women, of course, were not alone in an interest in personal grooming. Products to 'restore' women's hair generally offered a volumising effect, or even grey coverage, as was the case with 'Mrs S.A. Allen's World Hair Restorer – It quickly changes grey or white hair to its natural colour. A perfect hair dressing, delicately perfumed. Never fails.' But for men, it was all about maintaining a full head of hair. And while there were plenty of large companies offering treatments and solutions to do just that, many of them based on creating a feeling of warmth on the scalp, there were also examples of enterprising small businessmen who wanted to get in on the burgeoning trade.

Like William Rippon, hairdresser of Francis Street, Spalding, in Lincolnshire who, in May 1911, placed the following advertisement in the *Lincolnshire Free Press*: 'DON'T GROW OLD, but face advancing years with a bottle of Rippon's Hair Restorer. Best on the market. 1s, 2s

6d and 4s 6d per bottle. (The larger bottle would cost approximately £30 at 2024 value)

It isn't clear whether Rippon had invented his own formula, or was simply own-labelling an established product. But presumably, since he did not become a millionaire on the proceeds, it was no more effective than any of the other formulas that promised the same 'miracle'. He did receive, however, a letter from 'a grateful patient in Kenilworth' who had been recommended Rippon's 'renowned hair restorer' by a friend. The correspondent's wife had given him a dose, mistaking it for his gout medicine. So great had been the relief in his symptoms that he had decided to keep taking it. Three large bottles later and his gout was gone. It was potent stuff indeed!

Fashion, too, had long been an area of interest in Britain, but it had really been accessible only to wealthier members of society. By the dawn of the Edwardian era, this had changed. A huge new middle class could now follow and indulge in the latest fashions – a fact that was reflected in the many new monthly women's magazines that entered the market.

Myra's Journal (founded in 1875 as *Myra's Journal of Dress and Fashion*) and *Weldon's Ladies' Journal* (established the same year) both contained dressmaking patterns among a content which was generally aimed at the middle-class readership, although also proved of interest to many women outside that demographic. *Myra's Journal* for September 1910, for example, contained patterns for a 'Smart Autumn Skirt', 'Smart House Blouse', 'Adaptable Blouse or Over Blouse', and a 'Girl's Art Over Dress' that could be made in linen and adapted to make an overall. At just 3d a month (between 1901 and 1912), it was affordable for most women. For a penny a title, *Myra's* also sold needlework instruction books on topics as diverse as 'Sequin and Jewel Embroidery', 'Stocking Knitting' and 'Woollen Comforts for Soldiers and Sailors'. Features of the monthly journal included subjects like 'New Early Autumn Coats', 'Beautiful Gowns for Country Visits', 'Small Brim Mid-Season Millinery', and a 'Utility Princess Tunic'. The magazine offered value for money with fifty-odd pages variously containing instructions on the making and wearing of fashions and hairstyles. It also covered cooking and household management, nursery notes, an 'employment bureau', home decoration, etiquette, a serialised story and 'free bargains pages'. There were even palmistry and graphology sections – readers were encouraged to submit an ink handprint, or sample of handwriting for analysis. By 1905, a dedicated health and beauty section had been introduced.

There were features on the latest news from the 'fashion centres' of the world – namely Paris and Vienna – correspondence pages and advertisements for various sewing items that the keen dressmaker might require. Should readers need reminding that this was an aspirational magazine, there was also an advertisement for Charles Heidsieck vintage champagnes.

In contrast, *The Lady* (founded in 1885) and *The Gentlewoman* (1890) were intended solely for a wealthier readership. In 1910, *The Gentlewoman*'s, forty-eight pages, which came out weekly on a Saturday, cost 6d an issue. Its masthead declared: 'Subscribed to by the cultured classes throughout the United Kingdom, India and British Colonies, and the United States of America.'

It called itself 'The Foremost Ladies' Paper – First in Interest – First in Influence – First in Fashions'. A wide range of advertisements give a clue to the anticipated lifestyles of its readership. On one front page alone were presented Scott Adie Ltd – 'clock maker to the Royal Family', with its range of 'travelling coats and gowns, carriage rugs, tartan plaids and Scotch Tweeds'; the Crown Perfumery and its 'Crown Lavender Salts' and 'famous Crab Apple Blossoms Perfume'. And, for those anticipating travel, 'Yanatas ... the only proved remedy for sea sickness', which was used by various members of European royalty; plus advertisements for the Empire Hotel in the Derbyshire spa town of Buxton, and the Royal Palace Hotel in Paris. Inside, P&O advertised its mail and passenger services, as well as 'pleasure cruises'. Amid advertisements for fur coats, travelling cases – as used by 'Their Majesties' – 'Highland Dress for boys', and Bird's Custard, reports on 'The Shootings of Scotland and Scottish Country Houses', a section on 'Shopping by Post', and an article on 'Leading Jewesses of Society' – were features on the fashions of the day both in Britain and on the Continent.

For those ordinary folk, unable to afford such a high-end journal, even local newspapers were getting in on the act. They were now peppered with advertisements for what the shops selling them called 'fashions', although this tended to refer to all ladies' clothing, whether or not it abided by the very latest trends. But, should she wish, any woman could find out just what was in fashion. In 1911 'By Our Own London Correspondent', as *Bristol's Western Daily Press* crowned Clara E. De Moleyns, reported on the latest 'Conceits of Fashion' in the capital. At the time of her writing she declared, 'There is a decided inclination for violets in millinery decoration ... always a sure sign of approaching spring.'

Although, in the aftermath of Queen Victoria's death there were far more important matters to occupy British minds than ever-changing fashion, it did not take too long before a new silhouette – in an 's-shape' came into fashion. Assisted by a gentler corset that pushed the chest forward and the hips back, reducing pressure on the waistline, this new silhouette permitted women more physical freedom. Curvier hips and fuller chests were also more desirable, and there was less emphasis on a youthful style – high fashion 'looks' were now mature and sophisticated.

There was more detail in the form of lace, pleats and ruffles. Sleeves were now gently puffed at the shoulder yet slenderly fit to the lower arm and finished with fancy cuffs with scalloping, flaring or pointed details at the wrist. There were draped sleeves, bell-shaped sleeves that fell away from the wrist and even a return to the leg-of-mutton sleeves of the previous century, although with more restraint.

Dresses were generally in two pieces – a skirt and separate matching bodice. Fitted jackets were popular too. Skirts began the century fitted close to the hip and flared out below the knee in a trumpet shape and were very long, sometimes sweeping the floor. Then a fuller, more circular skirt featuring pleats, and using more fabric, became popular. But by 1910 they had become slender once more – the whole 'look' altogether more linear. By the outbreak of the Great War, the most popular skirts were ankle length.

Accessories were a very important part of the Edwardian lady's attire. When outside, upper-class ladies wore hats, which became larger and more ostentatious as the decade progressed. There had long been a craze for decorating hats with huge feather plumes. Such was the passion for birds' feathers that, in the mid-1880s, Emily Williamson had established The Plumage League to oppose the use of feathers in hats. So great was the demand – a demand that was only fulfilled by killing masses of birds and plucking their feathers – that many beautiful species of birds faced near-extinction. In 1891 the group amalgamated with The Fin, Fur and Feather Folk (founded in Croydon by Eliza Phillips, Etta Lemon, Catherine Hall and Hannah Poland) and forming what would, in 1904, become the Royal Society for the Protection of Birds.

Gloves were less contentious and almost always worn. A parasol or umbrella was usually carried by upper-class ladies, both to protect against the elements and simply to look pretty.

There were changes, too, in colours. If the Victorians had been fond of sombre tones, this began to change once the period of enforced mourning was over. Lighter, more uplifting and cheerful colours became popular in women's fashion. Fabrics became softer and more flowing. Texture became an important element of fashion, with lace becoming heavier and embroidery details more ornate.

Few factory workers, labourers or laundresses could afford to completely indulge in purchasing the latest fashions. Practicality would always rule. But they made an effort to modernise existing items using the sewing skills taught to them in schools or passed on to them by mothers and grandmothers. And most, regardless of social status, either invested in at least one new hat each year, or made alterations to their old one.

Newspapers, periodicals and advertisements exposed most people, in some way, to the latest styles and lifestyles. Although it would be some years before British women would become legally emancipated and regularly seen taking on roles outside the home, they already had access to an increasing variety of pastimes and physical activities. This was even more the case in the United States where Charles Dana Gibson's line drawings of beautiful, young, tall, athletic and ultra-feminine women were being used in countless advertisements and newspaper illustrations. These images quickly became works of art in their own right, and the so-called 'Gibson Girl' also became a familiar icon to people on this side of the Atlantic.

Gibson counted notable beauties like Camille Clifford and Evelyn Nesbitt among his models. The Gibson Girl, her hair pulled up on top of her head in a voluminous pompadour and fastened into a bun, could be seen on the beach with her friends, or on the golf course surrounded by admiring gentlemen, enjoying the countryside or garden, or playing a violin, often dressed in an outfit suited to the activity.

Many of the images were offered for sale in Britain in a series of picture postcards, divided into a number of themes. In 1907 they were offered through the pages of the *South London Press* with titles like 'The Man She Really Cares For' and 'Their First Quarrel', 'The Ancient and Honourable Game' and 'Is A Caddie Always Necessary?', and 'All is Vanity' and 'I Wish I Was A Dog'.

As 'free' a lifestyle as the Gibson Girl would appear to have, it was something of an illusion. First, she wasn't a real person, but an ideal specifically intended to be reflective of modern women. She became something of a symbol of progressiveness, without actually being all that progressive. She was not regarded as a challenge to the social status quo on either side of the Atlantic. This was no form of feminism. Quite the opposite. No Gibson Girl would ever be shown as a suffragette. She was simply an active, modern woman who now had access to more leisure choices and clothing more suited to those activities. For actual liberation, there was a long and difficult struggle to come.

Gradual social change saw men's sartorial fashion alter too. Three-piece suits, with long jackets and narrow trousers became de rigeur, with the belted single-breasted tweed Norfolk jacket, or a blazer, a popular choice for leisure time. Men's hairstyles were generally neat and slicked into place using hair oils made from caster, coconut, olive or almond oil. Scented 'Macassar' was a particularly popular solution. Its texture made it difficult to remove from fabric surfaces, giving rise to the popularity of the 'anti-Macassar' – a small piece of fabric placed over the back of a settee or armchair to provide a barrier between oiled-back hair and upholstery.

If the Macassar was an obvious outward sign of men's grooming, then women were still a little reticent to be seen indulging in too many beauty products. There was still something of a dividing line between products that were beneficial to a healthy appearance, and those which purely decorated the appearance. However, this began to change rapidly from March 1909 after the opening of one of Britain's biggest, and most forward-looking, businesses – the huge Selfridge & Co department store in London. And, for the first time, one of the biggest and most prominent departments in a store was devoted to female beauty.

American Harry Gordon Selfridge had spent twenty-five years working his way almost to the top at Marshall Field department store in Chicago. Thanks to his hard work and innovation he had reached the position of junior partner, but realising his name was never going to be incorporated into that of the store, he began to look elsewhere. According to the *Ottawa Free Press*, Selfridge retired from that position in 1904 with a fortune of $2 million (worth $69 million in 2024). Having visited London with his wife, he had been surprised that, given the size and importance of the city, it did not have a department store as impressive as those in Paris, or even Chicago. He was 51 years old and very much in need of a new project. He invested a remarkable £400,000 (worth more than £60 million in 2024) in building a huge new steel-framed department store – only the second such construction in London after The Ritz, and which would be partially responsible for changes made to London's building regulations. The steel structure allowed for huge windows around the outside of the building, and, with no need for multiple internal supporting walls, vast sales spaces within. As modern as its construction methods were, the exterior was clad in brick and plaster with huge classical columns and, as gargantuan as it was, Selfridges blended in with many of London's Georgian buildings. It was the second largest shop in the United Kingdom after Harrods and was ready for opening after only a few months' work.

Standing at the then unfashionable west end of Oxford Street, between Duke Street and Orchard Street, and just opposite an entrance to Bond Street tube station. 'Nine Smooth-running Electric Lifts' took customers between the eight floors – three were below street level. It was claimed that 'six miles of yard-wide Wilton Pile carpet' had been laid across a hundred different departments.

Selfridges opened with a great whirl of publicity, a queue of customers that wrapped around the store kept under control by thirty Metropolitan

Police officers, and the – then unique – notion that shopping could be a pleasurable leisure activity rather than a burden.

The store's interior was designed so that customers could see the products in attractive displays, rather than have to ask what was available. No beams to obstruct customers' views – only the occasional piece of the steel frame, cunningly disguised as another classical pillar. There were restaurants, reading rooms, a library, 'National Rooms' with registers for visitors, a 'First-Aid Ward with trained nurse in attendance', and even a 'Silence Room'. On the roof there was a garden which was utilised for special events. Customers could purchase railway, steamship and theatre tickets, and there was a Bureau de Change. Everything was designed to encourage customers to stay within the store's walls for as long as possible. Not for Selfridges, the usual London department store habit of having a customer escorted between departments by a 'walker' who had greeted them at the door. Customers would be encouraged to wander at will. If they did not choose to make a purchase that day, then Harry Selfridge reasoned that they soon would. And then there were the staff – some 1,200 of them. They were, according to publicity material, 'adequately salaried' and so gratuities from grateful customers were not permitted. Instead of simply serving customers, they were there to assist them, advise them and gently encourage them to buy. This element was of particular importance in the store's new beauty department, where perfume counters were stationed by the doors both to attract passers-by and to counteract potential ill-natured whiffs from the largely horse-drawn traffic, or less than hygienic customers – Selfridges was open to 'all'. Customers could openly seek individual advice from the staff, and watch demonstrations of the products, or even try before they purchased. Up to that point the wearing of makeup was not considered appropriate in polite society – at least, when the makeup was obvious. That was something associated with actresses and, worse still, prostitutes. While other shops might well sell such preparations, this had always been out of sight and in private. Selfridges' policy, however, made it possible for female customers to see cosmetics products in action. There was nothing too outrageous available – fashion decreed that the natural look was always the aim but, for the first time, gentle cosmetic enhancements were given tacit approval – adding a light rosy flush to the cheeks or deepening the tone of the lips with a daring red, enhancing the eyes or grooming the brows into shape. It would be some years before noticeable makeup became universally socially acceptable but, thanks to Harry Selfridge, it was now something women could talk about – even if it was only among their immediate social circle.

Selfridge was also a master of public relations. The store was constantly advertising in national newspapers, often filling whole pages with themed sales pitches. His suggestion that a direct subway link to Bond Street Tube station be built, and the station renamed 'Selfridges', was turned down, but Selfridges changed the face of British high streets by pioneering artistic window displays which were lit up each evening until after midnight. He continued to astound and attract the public with personal appearances by celebrities of the day. For four days in July 1909, after he had made the first cross-Channel flight, Louis Bleriot permitted his monoplane to be put on show at Selfridges', attracting tens of thousands of extra visitors to the store.

And, in possibly nothing short of a stroke of genius, in March 1910, after a Suffragette protest saw a number of Oxford Street properties come under attack, Selfridge pointedly refused to press charges against what he called 'the young lady who broke one of the store's famous windows'. Instead, he declared the store in full solidarity with the Suffragettes, created window displays in support of the cause and even flew the Suffragette flag from the store's roof. Reinforcing the idea that Selfridges was the modern store, he immediately placed advertisements acknowledging Christabel Pankhurst's assertion that 'Suffragettes must not be dowdy', and noting that his store sold 'the most powerful symbol of female emancipation: red lipstick ... as the first department store to sell lipstick, powder and rouge, Selfridges is leading the way for the country's Suffragettes'.

It was canny marketing, for certain, but it also ensured that no further damage was inflicted by protestors. Something that, as the fight for women's suffrage became more organised, and more radical, other business owners would have done well to follow.

CHAPTER 11

THE BATTLE OF SHEPHERD'S BUSH

> Though the immediate spectacle in the Stadium was marred by one of the untoward intervals of a glorious summer, we cannot doubt that yesterday's inaugural ceremony by the King was the stately prelude to magnificent success ... The fascinating thing about the Olympiads of the present and the future ought to be the very fact that they sift out of the general gathering the special aptitude of each nation.
>
> *Daily Telegraph*,
> 14 July 1908

That London staged its first Olympic Games thanks in part to the temperamental nature of an Italian volcano should have been portent enough: those 1908 Games, the fourth modern Olympiad, held in a Britain trying to throw off the repressions of the Victorian age, were not only the wettest in history, they were also probably the most contentious.

London stepped in to stage the Games after the eruption of Mount Vesuvius two years earlier meant that the Italian authorities, who were preparing infrastructure for the Olympic Games in Rome, had to divert funds for the reconstruction of the devastated city of Naples instead. In fact, the Italian government did not really want the Games in the first place, and in many respects, London was the ideal solution. More than any other country, Britain had much more collective experience in organising large sports events, with the Henley Royal Regatta, the

All-England (Wimbledon) tennis tournament, and the thirty-year-old Amateur Athletic Association's national track and field championships.

Baron Pierre de Coubertin, the 'father' of the modern Olympics, called upon a British friend, Lord Desborough, a former Liberal and then Conservative MP who had been raised to the peerage in 1905. Desborough had a fine sporting pedigree. He had rowed for Oxford in 1877 (the fabled dead heat) and 1878 University Boat Races, won the silver medal for fencing at the 1906 Intercalated Games (considered at the time as an Olympics). Swimming the Niagara rapids twice, climbing the Matterhorn three times and rowing across the English Channel in an eight were also among his many feats. He would also serve as president of the MCC, the All-England Lawn Tennis Club and the Amateur Fencing Association. He became an MP at the age of 25, and was offered the governor-generalship of Canada, which he declined.

Desborough was just the man to galvanise support for London to step in and, at short notice, stage an Olympic Games. The approach was made when he was in Athens for the 1906 Games. Britain already had an Olympic Association and with the help of its secretary and Desborough's friend, the Reverend Robert Stuart de Courcy Laffan, that organisation became the British Olympic Council (BOC) which would prove remarkably effective in organising the London Games.

The BOC could look back to the shambles of the 1900 and 1904 Games – when both Olympics were considered simply sporting sideshows to World Fairs – and take heart that there were so many lessons to be learned from the debacles of Paris and St Louis, the chaos of both still fresh in the memory. In Paris there had been no running track, competitors had outnumbered spectators, and the French and Americans had spent most of the time falling out with each other. Great Britain decided not to send even one competitor to St Louis in 1904. It proved a wise decision. Almost every day was marred by protest and counter-protest. The BOC was determined to set new standards. Had the debacles of the 1900 and 1904 Games been repeated in London, then the Olympic Games may have foundered there and then. So, for all their controversy and continued animosity between nations, it can be argued that the London Games of 1908 actually set the Olympic movement truly on its way.

Perhaps the BOC's greatest achievement was persuading the organisers of the 1908 Franco-British Exhibition, held to further the entente cordiale reached by Britain and France in 1904, to build a new stadium next door, complete with running and cycle tracks.

The exhibition itself would be held on a 140-acre site in Shepherd's Bush in West London. Its brilliant white plaster buildings earning the area the enduring name of the White City. Its organisers agreed that not only would they pay for the entire costs of a 93,000-capacity stadium (63,000 of them seated) – estimated at not less than £44,000 (£6.9 million at 2024 value), it was reported – but they would also grant the BOC £2,000 (£314,000) towards the cost of staging the Olympics. In return they would receive 75 per cent of the gate receipts. It was later reported that the cost of the stadium rose to £220,000 (34.5 million), and the BOC grant to £20,000 (£3.14 million)).

The White City Stadium – the first purpose-built Olympic stadium – was completed in only ten months and was considered to be a technological marvel for the time. Meanwhile, a public appeal for contributions towards the day-to-day running costs of the Games was less successful; by the end June it had raised less than £3,000 (£471,000) from 200 subscribers, most of them friends of Lord Desborough. Before the opening ceremony a further £10,000 (1.57 million) was needed. 'We need money to entertain our visitors,' said the assistant secretary of the BOC, adding, 'Visitors from England, be they athletes or schoolmasters, are always received royally abroad.'

Lord Northcliffe, owner of the *Daily Mail*, reluctantly agreed that the newspaper would sponsor a final appeal. It proved a remarkable success, raising almost £16,000 (£2.51 million) and including the Prince of Wales and the American millionaire Cornelius Vanderbilt in its list of donors. Canadian dancer Maud Allan, noted for her Dance of the Seven Veils, donated the proceeds of a special matinee performance at the Palace Theatre in the West End. Even the French government chipped in with £680 (£107,000).

The cinder running track (three laps to a mile), measured 586.67yds (536.44m). A banked cycling track measured 660yds (603.5m), and there was a swimming pool 100m in length. Soccer, rugby union, hockey and lacrosse would be played inside the running track, archery was held on the grass infield and there were platforms for wrestling and gymnastics, and so spectators could watch the athletics events and other sports at the same time. The stadium was years ahead of its time and was used as a model for the one that was built in Berlin, at the Grunewald racecourse, for the 1916 Games which, of course, were never staged.

Besides the Royal Box, the Franco-British Exhibition, the International Olympic Committee, the BOC and the Comité d'Honneur, which comprised three representatives from each competing country, each had their own box. As for the Royal Box, there was just over a week to go before Edward VII finally agreed to attend the opening ceremony. Travelling from Buckingham Palace by horse-drawn carriage, the King and Queen entered the stadium at just before 3.50pm on Monday 13 July. They were joined by the Prince and Princess of Wales – the Prince only just made it after a police constable did not recognise him and tried to direct who he thought was 'an unprivileged intruder' into the public area; fortunately the officer's mistake was pointed out before an incident could develop – as well as two of their other sons, Princess Victoria, the Duke and Duchess of Connaught and Princess Patricia, the Crown Prince and Princess of Greece and their children, the Duke and Duchess of Argyll, the Crown Princess of Sweden, and the Maharajah of Nepal.

A planned demonstration by some unemployed men, who wanted to hand a petition to the King on his way to the White City, had been cancelled due to the heavy rain, and now, with the words, 'I declare the Olympic Games of London open', the King signalled the beginning of two weeks of competition, controversy and bad weather.

On that opening day spectators were treated to athletics, swimming, gymnastics and cycling events, but perhaps the most intriguing was the late afternoon's demonstration sport, a bicycle polo match between the German Cycling Federation and the Irish Bicycle Polo Association. The Irish won the six-a-side contest, played over four chukkas, or quarters, 1-0.

The Daily Chronicle reported:

> The Olympic Games of London were yesterday declared open by the King, and there ensued forthwith 'the striving

of swift feet and strong bodies', which was the glory of the Olympic Games of Ancient Greece. The march past the King of the competing athletes suggests one vital difference between this revived festival and its prototype. The old Olympic Games were essentially a national festival, a patriotic gathering of Hellenes. such they endured for twelve centuries, surviving even the extinction of Greek freedom. In their reincarnation after fourteen centuries they have become a great international festival. Many and diverse were the national flags which dipped to the salute in the 'Stadium' at Shepherd's Bush yesterday. Let us hope that in their enlarged scope the Games will be effective, even as were those of old, in promoting some sense of solidarity among those who partake in them. The international idea may well be encouraged by these friendly contests in innocent rivalries.

The *Daily Mirror* thought that the 'most captivating' sight of all was a gymnastics display by some Danish girls: 'They looked charming in their cream blouses and short divided skirts, with brown stockings and shoes.'

The newspaper also commented on the fact that the stadium was barely half full of spectators, leaving 'huge gaps in the vast amphitheatre': 'It is to be hoped that there will be much better attendances in the fortnight to come. Large empty spaces in the seating must have a depressing effect on the competitors as well as the spectators.'

The 1908 Games were played out under continually rainy skies and suffered from endless arguments between British officials and those of the many other countries involved – especially the United States, with whom there was enormous animosity.

The 'Battle of Shepherd's Bush', as it became known, began almost immediately, when the US delegation noticed that there was no American flag flying in the stadium at the opening ceremony. It was then alleged that US flag bearer and discus champion, giant shot-putter Ralph Rose, responded by refusing to dip the Stars and Stripes when he passed

King Edward VII's box. Ironically, some American citizens had been in charge of decorating the stadium.

Those responsible for flying the flags had got themselves into something of a tangle. It was not only the Stars and Stripes that was missing. The flag of another competing nation, Sweden, was also conspicuous by its absence, while the flags of China and Japan fluttered in the wind, despite the fact that neither nation was taking part. The Finns, meanwhile, had been refused permission to fly their flag when the Russians objected because the Grand Duchy of Finland was still considered part of Russia. The Finns refused to march under the Russian flag, instead joining the parade led only by a standard bearer.

These were far from the only controversies surrounding the 1908 Olympic Games, although no one foresaw the biggest of them all. 'No event in the athletic history of Great Britain has aroused so much public enthusiasm', was how the *Daily Telegraph* described the 1908 Games. And the marathon, according to the newspaper, would be the highlight of a crowning day when 'twenty-two different nations are represented in an amicable contest which reminds us that, by slow and sure degrees, civilisation is moving towards the friendly federation of mankind'.

When one considers the conflicts yet to come, never mind the politics that would inexorably be bound with future Olympic Games, these were lofty ideals – and there had been lessons already unlearned. Like the 1904 Olympics in St Louis when, nine miles into the marathon, American runner Fred Lorz, stricken with cramp, accepted a lift in his manager's car. Alas, in those early days of the internal combustion engine, rides in such vehicles were not always destined to end in quite the right place, and, with five miles to go, the car broke down and Lorz was obliged to alight and finish his journey on foot. Now refreshed, he trotted nimbly into the arena to accept the cheers of his fellow countrymen. It was only when the US President's daughter, Alice Roosevelt, appeared to congratulate him that the truth came out. The American Athletic Union handed Lorz a lifetime ban. Meanwhile, as Lorz was running full of vigour into the stadium, British-American Thomas Hicks had been staggering blindly along in second place, helped by egg whites, brandy, water – and even a dose of strychnine. With Lorz disqualified, Hicks was awarded the gold medal, although his efforts almost cost him his life. Lorz was soon forgiven and the following year won the Boston marathon.

Four years later in 1908 – and quite by accident – the standard marathon distance was established after the starting line was moved from its planned location to Windsor Castle in order to give the royal family a better view, and for it to finish in front of the Royal Box at the White City; this marathon too ended in chaos. The race had begun at just after 2.30pm on 24 July, when the Princess of Wales gave the signal for fifty-six athletes representing sixteen countries (not twenty-two as the *Daily Telegraph* had reported) set off out through the Sovereign's Gate at a blistering pace and under a blazing sun.

When the leader, Dorando Pietri, a 23-year-old confectioner from Capri, finally staggered into the packed stadium he took a wrong turn and began running in the opposite direction before being called back; he collapsed, was helped up by attendants and even by spectators, wobbled and fell three more times before being half-carried across the finish line.

Initially declared the winner just as the second-placed runner, Johnny Hayes of the US, entered the stadium, the Italian was inevitably disqualified in favour of Hayes, but only after British and American officials had argued for an hour and fights had broken out in the stands.

In the 400 metres final, there were only four runners – three Americans and a Briton – and when the American winner, John Carpenter, was disqualified by British judges, who ordered a re-run, Carpenter's colleagues, William Robbins and John B. Taylor, refused to take part, leaving the Briton, Wyndham Halswelle, a Highland Light Infantry officer who had served in the Second Boer War, to run around the track alone to take the gold medal. Captain Halswelle was killed by a sniper's bullet during the Battle of Neuve Chappelle in March 1915, while attempting to rescue an injured fellow officer.

The USA also refused to continue in the best-of-three tug-of-war quarter-final after being defeated by a team of Liverpool policemen who represented Britain. The Americans claimed that the police were wearing footwear in violation of a rule against 'projecting nails, tips, sprigs, points, hollows or projections of any kind'.

The Americans complained about the method of drawing heats for the athletics races, claiming that their runners were being drawn together, which would give only one American per heat the opportunity to advance.

In the high jump and pole vault, the Americans protested that no soft-landing pit was available, and then they claimed that the early rounds should be restaged after the rest of the competition was moved to more favourable conditions.

In the pole vault, the Americans were upset again, this time because no hole was provided for placement of the pole.

Other countries also complained. Both Canada and France complained bitterly about what they felt were unfair decisions in cycling. In the rugby union tournament, the British team (represented entirely by county champions Cornwall), soundly beaten by Australia, 32-3, protested that their opponents had been wearing dangerous spikes. Both teams had gone straight into the final after France – the only other nation to enter the rugby competition – were unable to raise a team.

When Irish athletes were compelled to compete for the Great Britain team, many of them withdrew due to the Home Rule crisis.

Yet the British organisers had brought considerably more order to the Olympics, primarily by limiting the number of athletes that could represent any one country in a given event.

London also set a standard for future international swimming competition by building that 100-metre pool, clearly marked into lanes.

Unusually, the 1908 London Olympics began on 27 April but were largely decided in two two-week periods, one in July, and one in October, when the British planted the seed of the future Winter Olympics by adding figure skating to the programme. (Two other new sports, powerboat racing and the tug-of-war, were never again seen in the Olympics).

There were many highlights. Swedish Olympian Oscar Swahn, at 60, was the oldest ever competitor to earn an Olympic gold medal, won the running deer shooting, single shot.

American Ray Ewry won the standing high jump and the standing long jump for the third time and became the only person in Olympic history to win a career total of eight gold medals in individual events.

And in the spirit of sportsmanship, the final of the middleweight Greco-Roman wrestling between Sweden's Frithiof Martensson and his fellow countryman Mauritz Andersson was postponed one day to allow Martensson to recover from a minor injury. Martensson won.

Forty-four nations took part in the 1908 London Olympics. The 2,023 competitors, of whom only forty-four were women, competed in 109 medal events. Great Britain fielded 676 competitors, almost twice as many as their closest rival France (363 athletes) and more than five times as many as America (121 athletes). Not surprisingly, Britain topped the medals table with a total of fifty-six Gold, fifty-one Silver and thirty-nine Bronze.

Of the closing ceremony on Saturday, 25 July, the *Western Times* reported:

> Although the gathering was poorly patronised in its earlier stages, the past four days have brought out record crowds ... There was an enormous gathering for the final scene of the Olympic Games. The Queen and Princess Victoria motored down, arriving at four o-clock. Parts of the stadium were packed and seats generally were well filled. The Royal party arrived without ceremony ... The Crown Prince of Sweden was in the Royal Box. The American ambassador and the Italian ambassador were presented ... At 4.30pm a procession of winners past the Royal Box was heralded by the playing of See The Conquering Hero Comes by the Grenadiers band and drum role as the Queen advanced to distribute prizes ... The demonstration of the day was reserved for Dorando, the disqualified Italian in the Marathon Race. He advanced to the dais carrying the Italian flag to thunderous cheers. The Queen heartily congratulated him in handing him her handsome silver cup [her own personal gift].

The name of Dorando Pietri would live on long after most people had forgotten the name of the winner of the 1908 Olympic marathon. He even inspired Irving Berlin to write a song entitled *Dorando* in 1909. It contains the lyrics, 'Dorando! Dorando! He run-a, run-a, run-a, run like anything.'

The day after the race, *The Mail* commented:

> This little Italian confectioner, 24 hours ago a pitiable tottering wreck, looking like an old man on the brink of the grave, but now a quiet, self-possessed sturdy young man, was the hero of the multitude. A mighty roar went up as he made his way to the tail-end of the procession of prize winners, and the shouts and cheers and cries of applause and sympathy were renewed again and again when it came to his turn to climb up the broad red-carpeted steps, placed almost exactly where he had fallen for the last time at the end of his gallant struggle ... Not even the cheers which hailed the winner of the race ... could compare in volume and cordiality with those that were now Dorando's recompense ... Verily we are a strange nation.

On the Sunday following the closing ceremony, Lord and Lady Michelham – Lord Michelham was the financier, philanthropist and member of the Stern banking family who had been ennobled in 1905 – gave a party at their Twickenham home, Strawberry Hill House – Britain's finest example of Gothic revival architecture – for 2,000 competitors and officials of the London Olympics Games. According to the *Kilkenny Moderator*, 'this international gathering was a brilliant success'.

Among the guests was Johnny Douglas, a future England cricket captain, who had also won Olympic gold as the 1908 middleweight boxing champion. This was the era of cricketers like W.G. Grace, whose career had begun when Victoria's reign still had thirty-six years to run, and ended seven years after Edward VII ascended the throne. There were many other colourful cricketers, of course, none more so than the tall, slim, right-handed Reginald Herbert Spooner, one of the most stylish batsmen of this, cricket's 'Golden Era'. Reggie Spooner served with the Manchester Regiment during the Second Boer War and recovered from enteric fever to become perhaps the greatest batsman of the Edwardian Era. He played in ten Test matches for England, seven of them against Australia. In the First World War he served as a captain in the Lincolnshire Regiment and was twice severely wounded. He was one of those gloriously multi-talented sportsmen of his time, and in January 1903 represented England at Rugby Union against Wales at Swansea.

The first London Olympics also saw the first brother and sister medallists. William Dod won gold in the men's archery competition, and his sibling, Charlotte ('Lottie') took silver in the women's event. The years leading up to the First World saw a remarkable cast of British sporting personalities, none more so than the Dods, four siblings – Lottie, Willie, Annie and Tony – members of a wealthy Cheshire family. Annie was a good golfer and billiards and tennis player, and an excellent ice skater. Tony excelled at archery, tennis and chess. Willie, of course, was an Olympic archery gold medallist.

It was Lottie, though, who had become a household name long before the London Olympics. She can be justifiably regarded as one of the first female sporting superstars.

Her first love was tennis, which she played in what was described as an aggressive style. In 1887 she became the youngest player to win a singles event at Wimbledon at the age of 15, a record which stands to this day. By the time she had retired from the game aged 21 she had won four more Wimbledon singles titles, and earned the press soubriquet 'The Little Wonder'. Throughout her tennis career she had few rivals and won every single match she played for three years. In the still young sport of lawn tennis, she had little left to achieve. Lottie began to seek challenges in other sports. She took up golf and won the 1904 Ladies British Open Amateur Championship, beating May Hezlet by one hole in the final at Troon, an event marred by what newspapers described as 'a perfect rabble' when some of the 5,000 crowd – the attendance was swelled by the afternoon closure of the Troon shipyard and local shops – 'rushed all over the course'.

Lottie also played field hockey – representing England twice, having helped to found the national team. She took up ice skating and, in 1895, passed the St Moritz Ladies' Skating Test, the most prestigious figure skating event for women at the time. The following year she became only the second woman to pass the men's test. She tobogganed down the Cresta Run and then she and Tony took up mountaineering, and scaled some of Europe's most challenging peaks. Lottie took up bobsledding, curling and ice hockey too, and became an expert rower and horse-rider. After the Olympics, she trained in first-aid and home nursing and served with the Voluntary Aid Detachment during the First World War.

CHAPTER 12

DOWN AT THE OLD BULL AND BUSH

> They don't pay their sixpences and shillings at a music hall to hear the Salvation Army. If I was to try to sing highly moral songs, they would fire ginger beer bottles and beer mugs at me. I can't help it if people want to turn and twist my meaning.
>
> Marie Lloyd

One Saturday morning in September 1906 the citizens of London were transfixed by tales of a bear hunt through the streets of the city. The unfortunate creature was named Philip and was the regimental 'pet' of the 2nd Life Guards based in London. The 2-year-old American black bear had lived with the regiment since he was a cub. He was reputedly tame to the point of following the soldiers around if they offered him a biscuit. He played gently with visiting children and was reported never to have bitten or attacked anyone.

However, this was soon to change. Philip had become too large for his quarters and so was now on his way to a new home at Dublin Zoo. He was locked in a special travelling cage, which was to be carried on a horse-drawn railway van from the Albany Street Barracks at Regent's Park to Euston Station. Surrounded by many of the soldiers, who had come to wave off their beloved mascot, Philip became agitated and clawed at the cage, roaring. As the vehicle travelled along Euston Road, Philip became more distressed and got his claws caught in the ventilation hatches, eventually managing to wrench one of the sides off the cage. The terrified bear leapt from the vehicle and made off down Argyle Street, and along Gray's Inn Road, pursued by a mob which struggled to keep up. Their shouts of warning to members of the public startled the bear even more and he escaped into the saloon bar of the Pindar of Wakefield pub at No 328. Perhaps the bear knew that a pinder is an historic term for someone employed to impound stray or escaped animals because, in just a few minutes inside the pub, the bear managed to overturn tables and smash glasses. Back outside the bear bit a boy named Charles Mailes as he tried to grab the bruin. Philip took refuge in nearby gardens where he was surrounded by 'hunters' armed with lassos, and who struggled to nab him as he sped from garden to garden crashing into boundary fences as he went. In his panic Philip bit one of his pursuers on the leg and several others on the hands. Eventually a group of around thirty police constables managed to surround Philip and throw a large net over him. The bear continued to roar his anger while being transported to the nearby King's Cross Road Police Station, where he was given a meal of dog biscuits and locked in a cell overnight. He was returned to his barracks while a stronger travelling cage was constructed.

His adventure was followed closely by newspaper readers. After all, escaped bears were a rare – probably unique – occurrence, even in London. In general, Edwardian Britons had to rely on more pre-organised events for their amusement – and new technologies were providing new forms of entertainment. While variety and music hall, now often lit by electricity rather than gas, remained the most popular, people were beginning to embrace the latest technological wonder – moving pictures. While cinema had been available to the public for only a few years, there was already a public hunger to see the latest offerings. Many theatres, if not turning over entire evenings of entertainment to the fledgling art form, often included a cinematic element in their latest shows. Typical was the bill at the Liverpool Empire of 27 August 1907, when well-known artist George Lashwood 'the Beau Brummel of the Variety Stage' topped the bill. He was ably supported by Florence Lambert and Robert Robinson in a sketch entitled 'Scots Folk Wooin'', and which featured the popular song *Annie Laurie*. There were various dancers and acrobatic troupes, and Herbert Clifton 'the marvellous voiced mimic', who would make a good career performing on both sides of the Atlantic to audiences that included kings and presidents. Possessed of an impressive vocal range, Clifton would find his greatest success working as a noted 'feminine impersonator'. The *Liverpool Daily Post* reviewed the entire bill and noted that the accompanying 'Bioscope pictures are, as usual, very interesting'.

Bioscope was just one of several companies which had launched their own cinema systems since 1896 – when the Lumiere Brothers opened their first Cinematographe in London. Robert Paul's Theatrograph (later renamed the Animatagraphe) and the American Biograph were among the others. As well as theatres and lecture halls even schools became locations for regular screenings.

On Wednesday, 7 February 1900, in the tiny Board School in the small Derbyshire village of Mickleover – a few miles to the west of Derby – Britain's first children's matinee performance had taken place, prior to a screening for adults.

From the middle of the decade dedicated picture houses were opened. The Daily Bioscope, which was a subsidiary of the Gaumont company, was possibly the first permanent one in Britain, being converted from two large shops in Bishopsgate, London, just opposite Liverpool Street Station. It opened in May 1906 and, for 4d or 2d each, an audience of up to 130 could view 20–30-minute repeating shows of the latest 'world events'. The first performance showed the aftermath of the recent San Francisco earthquake and sporting action from the Athens Olympics of 1896, all explained by what the *Morning Leader* called 'a mysterious voice concealed behind the darkness'. Other early events shown were the Epsom Derby of that year, and the wedding of Princess Victoria Eugenie – the niece of Edward VII – and King Alfonso XIII of Spain. The first audiences were largely drawn from the local office workforce.

As the number of picture houses began to grow across the capital and out across the country, concerns were raised about the licensing, or rather lack of licensing, of the venues of this form of entertainment. In London, the county council (LCC) struggled to categorise the art form. It was not stage, nor music, nor dancing. Some shows did take place in premises already licensed for those purposes, but there were already twelve specialist cinemas, and 150 other venues regularly showing moving pictures.

The main concern was safety in these unregulated venues. In 1907 a fire at Newmarket town hall, caused when a bioscope projector was knocked over, killed three and injured many more. There were also concerns about the potential immorality of cinema. Particularly when dozens of young folk gathered together unsegregated, unchaperoned and in the dark. The superintendent of Southwark police station visited one venue at Borough in 1909 and became concerned that, because boys and girls were not separated in the auditorium, 'the place lends itself to indecent practices'.

The remarkable speed at which new cinemas were opening – by 1911 in London there were as many cinemas as theatres and music halls combined – alarmed many. There were twenty-seven, twenty-six and twenty-four in the boroughs of Wandsworth, Islington and Lambeth respectively. The LCC began to put pressure on the Home Office to introduce some sort of restrictions.

The Cinematograph Act of 1909, applying to all commercial cinemas – in other words anywhere the public paid for admission – did just that. Importantly, it required that the dangerous projection equipment be housed within a fire-resistant barrier. Those cinemas had to be inspected and licensed by their local authority. New regulations meant that it was often more cost-effective to build a cinema from scratch. The new law also gave local councils the right to grant or refuse licences based upon the content of films shown, which led to inadvertent censorship. The British Board of Film Censors was established in 1912 by cinema companies themselves. This was partly a response to the reaction to the 1912 American film *From the Manger to the Cross*, about the life of Jesus. Such was the indignation at the idea that a company might make a profit from such subject matter, that the film companies elected to create their own censorship controls, rather than have them enforced by the government.

Most films presented to the public, of course, were entirely without controversy. Companies like the Gaumont-British Picture Corp, founded in 1898, would eventually build their own studios at Lime Grove – the first in Britain built solely for film production. Ealing Studios – now the oldest continuously operating film studio in the world – was established in 1902 by Will Barker. Hepworth Studios opened in Lambeth, the Ideal Film Company started up in Soho in 1911, and Elstree Studios began work in 1914. But film production would take place all across the nation including in Yorkshire by the Bamforths, and in Wales under the watch of William Haggar.

Much of the content was news-based or documentary-style films about science, technology and discovery. But artistic forms and fictional subjects were becoming more popular, albeit at a slower pace. Films were short and entirely silent, often accompanied by live music played on the piano or by a small orchestra. Lack of sound did not mean a lack of imagination on behalf of film-makers. In 1901, Walter R. Booth's five-minute *Scrooge, or Marley's Ghost* became the earliest film adaptation of a Charles Dickins' work. Taking the form of 'twelve animated tableaux', it was shown, by royal command, at Sandringham, to the King and Queen who were no doubt impressed by special effects that saw a translucent ghost of Marley show Scrooge the error of his ways. Two years later, Cecil Hepworth and Percy Stow directed *Alice in Wonderland* – the first film adaptation of the Lewis Carroll book. Audiences must have been astonished as Alice grew and shrank according to what she ate and drank. In the same year Frank Mottershaw of Sheffield produced *A Daring Daylight Robbery* (sometimes *Burglary*), which featured cinema's first chase scene and included members of the Sheffield Fire Brigade and local music hall artistes in the cast. What is, reputedly, Britain's first animated film was Walter R. Booth's *The Hand of the Artist* (1906) which used sophisticated techniques like stop motion, an advanced form of flipbook-style animation.

Almost every picture house, regardless of the type of programme they offered, would show news-related items first. In June 1904, the *Weston-super-Mare Gazette and General Advertiser* reported that the town's Grand Pier and Pavilion would be showing several American Biograph pictures including one showing strongman and wrestler George Hackenschmidt in action, and another called *Life on Japanese*

Warships. Even general elections received the cinematic treatment. In 1910 the *Daily Record* announced that, along with screens showing the election results as they came in, it would be showing 'cinematograph and limelight shows which relieve the tedium of waiting for the results'.

In November 1912, the *Birmingham Mail* reported that the cinematograph might become 'an integral part of the elementary school equipment ... thousands of people are daily receiving in the picture palaces of the city valuable instruction in history, geography and science ...'. It argued that no school, no matter how well equipped, could hope to present the variety of experiments that were being shown via the 'cinematographic lantern'.

If the cinema, thanks to its low prices and widespread availability, was fast on its way to becoming the preferred entertainment of the masses in Edwardian Britain, literature and serious theatre still held a draw to the middle and aspiring classes.

Novelists of the new science fiction and fantasy genres, like H.G. Wells, were highly popular. By the end of 1914, the prolific writer had published twenty-four novels. Among the most successful were *The Time Machine, The Island of Doctor Moreau, The Invisible Man, War of the Worlds*, and *The First Men in the Moon*.

More classic themes were taken up by E.M. Forster, who wrote predominantly about society and interactions between the classes. H. Rider Haggard, most famous for *King Solomon's Mines*, remained popular throughout the Edwardian era. He wrote predominantly about life in the colonies from the white settlers' perspective, although he showed native characters a greater sympathy than was usual at the time. In contrast, John Galsworthy wrote largely about upper middle-class nouveau-riche families like his own. *A Man of Property* – the first book in his Forsyte Saga trilogy – was published in 1906.

To much public outcry one of the most popular authors of the entire Victorian Age, Arthur Conan Doyle, had killed off his famous character Sherlock Holmes in 1893. *The Final Problem* had Holmes and his rival Moriarty fall to their deaths down the Reichenbach Falls. Doyle realised there was still public hunger for more Holmes stories. In 1901 he unexpectedly revived Holmes in a new story *The Hound of the Baskervilles*. His miraculous survival – only Moriarty had fallen but Holmes had allowed his death to be reported to avoid other enemies – being explained in a new short story *The Adventure of the Empty House* published two years later. Doyle continued to write adventures for his fictional detective until 1927.

It was truly a golden age for children's literature. Beatrix Potter's first book *The Tale of Peter Rabbit* was published in 1902, with *The Tale of Squirrel Nutkin* and *The Tailor of Gloucester* following a year later. She continued to write, producing two or three books a year right up to the Great War. Other children's Edwardian favourites included E. Nesbitt with The *Wouldbegoods* (1901), *Five Children and It* (1902), *The Phoenix and the Carpet* (1904), and *The Railway Children* (1906); Rudyard Kipling's *Kim* (1901), *Just So Stories* (1902), *Puck of Pook's Hill* (1906) and *Rewards and Fairies* (1910); *The Wind in the Willows* by Kenneth Grahame (1908); and Frances Hodgson Burnett's *The Secret Garden* (first appeared in serialisation 1910).

J.M. Barrie had first used his character Peter Pan in the 1902 novel *The Little White Bird* to some literary success. But it was its transformation into the stage play *Peter Pan, or the Boy Who Wouldn't Grow Up* in 1904 which propelled it to the status of a classic. It premiered at London's Duke of York Theatre on 27 December 1904 to great acclaim. Newspaper reviews declared it to be 'A Christmas Fairy Tale to Suit Young and Old'. One London reporter noted: 'It held the audience from start to finish.'

Early in the century, London's Royal Court Theatre in Sloane Square began to concentrate on productions of modern drama, providing the perfect outlet for the works of Irish writer George Bernard Shaw, who was something of a political firebrand. Fourteen of his plays were put on at the Royal Court in the company's first few years. *Man and Superman*, *Major Barbara*, and *The Doctor's Dilemma* brought Shaw great international success. In 1912 his latest play *Pygmalion* premiered in Austria and Germany before the English language version opened on the London stage to great success. Its run was short – from April to July 1914 – but would certainly have been longer had its leading man, Sir Herbert Beerbohm Tree, appearing as professor of phonetics

Henry Higgins, not insisted on taking a holiday. His co-star, Mrs Patrick Campbell, as Cockney flower girl Eliza Doolittle, then took the play on a tour of the United States. Beerbohm Tree's illegitimate children included the film director Carol Reed, and he was the grandfather of the actor Oliver Reed.

Elsewhere in London, countless stages offered theatrical entertainment in all its variations. In one week alone in June 1902, the Royal Opera House at Covent Garden was performing *Carmen*, *Tannhauser*, *L'Elisir d'Amore*, *Pagliacci* and *Cavalleria Rusticana*. A night at the opera was expensive – the cheapest stalls tickets cost 5s (almost £40 at today's value). If you wanted a box, it would set you back as much as four guineas (more than £600 today).

Just two minutes' stroll away, at the Theatre Royal on Drury Lane, there was a remarkable staging of the 'Stupendous Production' of *Ben Hur*. It was an extraordinary spectacular. The great chariot race was re-enacted on the huge stage by, according to *The Era*, 'four great cradles, 20 feet in length and 14 feet wide, which are movable back and front on railways'. Real horses were able to gallop towards the audience at great speed because they were secured by invisible steel cables and running on concealed treadmills. Behind them a large cyclorama revolved in the opposite direction to create the illusion of even greater speed, while clouds of dust were blown to added effect by fans. *The Sketch* declared it 'thrilling and realistic', while the *Illustrated London News* called it 'a marvel of stage illusion ... memorable beyond all else'.

Most London theatres were content with standard productions. At the Lyceum, Henry Irving was leading the cast of *Faust* each evening, while also playing leading roles, alongside Ellen Terry, in *The Merchant of Venice* and *King Charles I* at matinees.

Elsewhere, at Her Majesty's Theatre, there was Shakespeare's *The Merry Wives of Windsor*; at the Adelphi Miss Olga Nethersole led the cast of the controversial *Sappho*; at the Lyric married couple Johnston Forbes-Robertson and Gertrude Elliott starred in *Mice and Men*; while at the Imperial Theatre, Westminster – where the lessee was none other than Lillie Langtry, former actress and one-time mistress of

Edward VII – *Everyman* was staged; at the Garrick Sarah Bernhardt performed in *Frou-Frou*; at the Duke of York's Theatre comedy play *The Gay Lord Quex*; while *A Country House* was on stage at the Criterion; at the Gaiety it was new musical comedy *The Toreador*.

Serious theatre was becoming an ever more popular art form and, in 1904, actor–manager Herbert Beerbohm Tree (in 1909 he would be knighted for his services to the theatre) founded the Academy of Dramatic Arts in rooms above His Majesty's Theatre in the West End. It received its royal charter in 1920.

New and almost-new productions were quickly finding their way to regional theatres too. The English adaptation of Franz Lehar's *The Merry Widow* had premiered in London as recently as June 1907, but by May 1909 was making its second run at the Theatre Royal in Halifax – part of an extensive British tour. Just across the road was the Palace Theatre, which had been opened in 1903, and featured a number of variety acts. As did another local theatre, the Grand. This was typical of most large towns where more than one theatre meant a wider variety of entertainment options. In Nottingham in March 1909, for example, the Theatre Royal had the visiting Mr George Alexander's company and its production of *The Builder of Bridges* – described on the bill as 'the attraction of the London season'. The following week Mr George Edwards's London company and its *The Dollar Princess* entertained, and the week after that saw the much anticipated visit of the famed Johnston Forbes-Robertson and Gertrude Elliott in *The Passing of the Third Floor Back*. The Theatre Royal was sandwiched between two variety theatres – the Empire – with 'the great Japanese novelty' O Hana San with 'beautiful oriental scenes'; Mr Norman Wrighton and his playlet *Wake Up England!*; The Achmed Ibrahim Troupe – the 'bounding marvels of the age ... ten real Bedouin Arabs'; and a Bioscope show of Wilbur Wright on his flying machine. This was supported by Charles Kitson and Rhoda Windrum in 'the screaming military contretemps The Cuckoo'; a 'blackface' act by dancer Billy Hobbs; Maudie Francis a comedian, dancer Bert Woodward, 'the steeple-chasing cyclist'; and Fred Earle – a comedian. At the Hippodrome, opened in 1908, was an equally varied mixture of live action and film in which Mr & Mrs Bob Fitzsimons presented a 'clever playlet', and included *Renoff and his Dancing Horse*, and animated pictures by the Barrascope showing an FA Cup tie between Nottingham Forest and Millwall.

In another part of the city was the Grand Theatre where *A Message from Mars* was playing. Eighteen miles away, in the town of Derby, the Grand Theatre, which often featured serious dramas, was presenting two performances nightly, at 7pm and 9pm of 'Five Sisters Warwick – Lady Continental Trick Cyclists', whose act was described as 'refined, clever, original and up-to-date'. Also on the bill were Barry Morris – a character comedian; Katos Komikal Kidgets in their 'Automatic Theatre'; vocalist and dancer Gwennie Morgan; The Four Netty Janowsky – acrobats and gymnasts; and Max Gruber and Miss Adelina with their performing elephant horse and pony.

The importance of these novelty acts, comedians, singers and dancers had never been greater. Variety entertainment was popular right across the country and with all classes of people. Some of their 'turns' might not have been highbrow, but they were now certainly 'legitimate'.

At its peak, around 1880, there were seventy-eight large music halls, and 300 smaller venues operating in London alone. The typical music hall bill included a familiar cast of characters; there were generally several singers – one of whom might be a 'swell', plus a singer of comedy songs, another specialising in sentimental airs and, perhaps, a singer of a classical aria, or a male or female impersonator. These were interspersed with so-called 'speciality acts', which included comedians, ventriloquists, adagio acts (a sort of mixture of dance and acrobatics), aerial acts, jugglers, animal acts, trick cyclists, magicians, knife throwers, and even demonstrations of wrestling.

On 1 July 1912, George V and Queen Mary joined their guests, and an audience of members of the public – some of whom who had begun queueing at 5am – at a packed house at the Palace Theatre on Shaftesbury Avenue for the 'Music hall Command' – the forerunner of countless Royal Command and Variety Performances since. The interior was decorated with an estimated three million rose blooms and thousands of electric lights to bring about a 'fairyland' feel.

The Pall Mall Gazette of that day described the acts on the bill:

> ... Barclay Gammon was well known as a Society entertainer before he came to the music halls ... the Palace Girls are a miniature ballet troupe formed by John Tiller, a Lancashire man with a wide reputation for organising similar companies ... Fanny Fields is an American Jewess ... she becomes a Dutch Girl, sings Dutch character songs ... and is a clever clog dancer ...

There was also a juggler who used billiard balls and cues, a mimic, an 'eccentric American dancer', a ventriloquist act, a quick-change artiste, a conjuror and 'Little Tich', who came from the so-called 'grotesque' type of act whose physical differences were viewed as part of the show. He was just 4ft 8in tall and had six digits on each hand. He was famed for his 'big boot' dance and a costume of baggy trousers, hat and walking cane that was said to later inspire Charlie Chaplin.

Acts which today would certainly be accused of cultural insensitivity or appropriation did not, in 1912, raise an eyebrow. The Bogannys, an English acrobatic group dressed as 'Chinamen' and used a set resembling an opium den. Then there was the 'black-face act' George Chirgwin. He was a veteran music hall performer, born to a circus family, and by then in his sixties. His entire career had been spent as a 'blackface' act, but in time his trademark white diamond around his right eye, his black body stocking topped with a frock coat, and his exaggerated stove pipe top hat made him an altogether more artistic version. His act was a mixture of songs – he could vary his voice from bass to falsetto and could even yodel – and banter, topical or political jokes and instrument playing. As his career progressed, his hat became taller and his shoes longer and he occasionally changed up his 'look' to reverse the black and white, or even to dress half in black, half in white.

There were also some very famous names. Comedian George Robey, Scottish singer Harry Lauder (who performed his famous hit *Roamin' in the Gloamin'*) and Russian ballet dancer Anna Pavlova were among the better-known stars performing.

Vesta Tilley was one of the most lauded music hall stars in the country. An 'incomparable male impersonator' known especially for her character 'Algy' in the song *Piccadilly Johnnie With The Little Glass Eye*.

According to most accounts, the king and queen – who were not normally patrons of variety theatre – greatly enjoyed themselves. Although Queen Mary's opinion on Vesta Tilley varied from newspaper to newspaper. For every one that noted the queen laughed out loud at Tilley's Algy character, another would note that the royal ladies in general did not approve of actresses appearing in masculine clothes.

Of course, with royalty present, this was a more genteel version of music hall which was known for its often raucous, bawdy and risqué nature. It had originated in the saloon bars of public houses as a side entertainment while patrons drank and ate. Its huge popularity moved it into purpose-built or converted music halls. By the twentieth century, while food and drink could be consumed, the emphasis had shifted firmly to pure entertainment. There were many different types of music hall. Some provided universally acceptable acts with only an almost pantomime nod to the naughty. Others were more suitable for adults. And some were the kind that women – even those from the working classes – or broader tastes tended not to patronise. Some music halls advertised nights where men were encouraged to bring along their 'other halves' – although this was often not always a serious invitation, but rather an indication that ladies would be available to provide professional company during the evening.

With hundreds of venues right across the country, there were thousands of acts touring the circuit. What the keen music hall fan wanted to see was one of the business's great stars. Dan Leno had become the most famous comedian of his generation – often appearing as a dame during pantomime season. He had toured regional theatres and was regarded as the one of the best pantomime dames but, by 1900, his health was in dramatic decline. Although he continued to work, he had struggled with his physical and mental health for years, possibly due to syphilis. He became a heavy drinker, and spent a considerable time at seaside resorts to 'recuperate'. After his death in 1904, crowds stood three deep for over three miles to watch his funeral procession.

Harry Champion was another favourite. He popularised a number of humorous songs like *Any Old Iron*, *I'm Henery the Eighth, I Am*, and *Boiled Beef and Carrots*. Gus Elen was one of the so-called 'coster comedians' who dressed as a market stallholder and performed routines about being a Cockney, often singing songs about working-class life such as *If It Wasn't For the 'Ahses Inbetween* and *Pretty Little Villa Down at Barking*. Elen was one of the industry's biggest earners and earned £250 a week in 1900, when the average UK yearly wage did not yet reach £70.

Florrie Forde was an Australian-born singer and one of the greatest stars of the music hall. Part of the Royal Command cast, among her most popular songs were *Oh, Oh Antonio*, *Has Anybody Here Seen Kelly?*, and *Down At the Old Bull and Bush* – all of which had strong choruses that were easy for audiences to sing along with.

The undoubted queen of the music hall era, though, was Marie Lloyd who, although she had been entertaining audiences since 1895, was still going strong. One of her most famous songs was *Don't Dilly Dally on the Way* – about doing a 'moonlight flit' to avoid paying the rent, and was first performed just after the Great War. While Lloyd was famous for songs like the sentimental *The Boy I Love Is Up in the Gallery*, it was her use of double entendre that particularly appealed to audiences. Read off the page the lyrics to many of her songs seemed quite innocuous, but add in Lloyd's trademark bawdy delivery, punctuated by knowing nods and winks, and songs like *She'd Never Had Her Ticket Punched Before* and *When I Take My Morning Promenade (Do You Think My Dress Is A Little Bit?)* sounded a lot less innocent. Her fans might have loved it, but the authorities were not so enamoured. Lloyd, however, always maintained that any immorality was in the minds of those who objected and, when called to perform her songs before the Vigilance Committee to prove her point, would always sing them without any hint of the saucy delivery. Lloyd understood her audience well and when required to change the lyrics to *I Sits Among the Cabbages and Peas*, she instead sang *I Sits Among the Cabbages and Leeks*. In 1913 Lloyd topped the bill at the then newly opened Portsmouth Coliseum – actually the refurbished Empire Palace Theatre – where 'the Queen of

Comediennes ... with New Songs and Paris Gowns' was supported by Alf Rover 'the famous eccentric', Three Morandinis, 'wonderful equilibrists and gymnasts', and Elsie Ray 'juvenile vocalist', among others. Lloyd died in 1922, aged 52, three days after collapsing on stage at the Empire Hall, Edmonton, while performing *It's A Bit Of A Ruin That Cromwell Knocked About A Bit.*

By appearing at more than one venue per night, and thus annoying theatre owners who tried to restrict their freedoms, the biggest stars of the music halls could make a lot of money The owners, meanwhile, further angered artistes by trying to force the low-paid acts, and stagehands, to work extra matinees without any increase in pay and this resulted in the music hall strike of 1907. It began at London's Holborn Empire on 22 January. Almost immediately, theatrical workers – most of whom were members of the Variety Artistes' Federation – across the capital and beyond joined the strike in support. Their action was funded by several of the more successful artistes like Marie Lloyd who, despite her considerable wealth, had never forgotten her roots. She said:

> We the stars can dictate our own terms. We are fighting not for ourselves, but for the poorer members of the profession, earning thirty shillings to £3 a week. For this they have to do double turns, and now matinees have been added as well ... I mean to back up the Federation in whatever steps are taken.

Lloyd even joined picket lines. She performed there to raise spirits, and joined fundraising efforts. This spirit, and that of her peers, was looked upon most favourably by British music hall fans. The *Birmingham Mail* commented:

> It is a rather fine thing to find them, quite unselfishly, throwing all the weight of their influence into the movement for securing better conditions of employment, both for the humbler members of their own craft, and for those still

more obscure workers who comprise the orchestra, or who labour with their hands behind the scenes.

The newspaper did, however, liken the Federation to 'a highwayman who suddenly points a pistol at the head of an unsuspecting traveller and orders him to stand and deliver on the spot'. The strike lasted for almost two weeks and, after arbitration, ended with most of the strikers' demands met, and a minimum wage and maximum working week established.

The music halls had survived industrial action and debates about public taste. But after the end of the Great War they had new competition – from dance bands with jazz, swing and big band music, and from a new more family-oriented variety bills. New rules that banned alcohol sales in auditoriums in some locations also impacted attendances. While some acts and music halls were able to rebrand for the variety age, others were not and, after the Edwardian Age, music hall entertainment fell by the wayside.

CHAPTER 13

OH, I DO LIKE TO BE BESIDE THE SEASIDE

> 'Well, it has been a grand day!'
> Unnamed employee of
> Burton's Bass Brewery,
> July 1906.

They came in their thousands. Men and women and youngsters. Most of them were employees of Messrs Bass, Ratcliffe & Gretton – the great brewing empire of Burton upon Trent.

Every fifteen minutes for three and a half hours, another train would pull up to a platform at Blackpool's Talbot Road Station (now Blackpool North) and another 500 or so excited day trippers would be disgorged into the seaside town.

Each one clutched the precious ticket that not only ensured their passage back to the East Midlands, but would permit them access to the resort's most enjoyable diversions.

It was July 1911, and some 8,000 workers, and their families, from the Bass Brewery had put down their tools for the day to enjoy an annual treat that Bass had been providing – free of charge – for its employees more or less every year since 1865.

Trips to the seaside, of course, were nothing new – since the eighteenth century Britons, particularly the wealthier members of society, had been travelling to the nation's coastal towns for the health-giving benefits of ocean bathing and fresh air.

The establishment of the railway network throughout the nineteenth century now made a seaside trip accessible to the vast majority of the population. The 1871 Bank Holidays Act had given workers an additional four or five days off. In England, Wales and Ireland these were Easter Monday, Whit Monday, the first Monday in August and Boxing Day; in Scotland they were New Year's Day, Good Friday, the first Monday in August and Christmas Day. By the early twentieth century there were regular newspaper advertisements for releases of building plots at would-be seaside resorts that were ripe for investment. One such was St Margaret's Bay, 'the rapidly rising seaside resort between Deal and Dover'. However, its narrow shingle beach, nestled beneath famous white chalk cliffs, was quite difficult to access and St Margaret's did not catch on in the way of other South Coast resorts.

Many factories and mills observed week-long shutdowns to give their employees a chance to take a holiday of sorts. These Wakes Weeks, as they were called in the North-West in particular, often found dozens of families from the area holidaying in the same resort.

And then there were companies like Bass, who not only gave their entire workforce an extra day off work, but transported them to the coast and put on entertainment and activities for their enjoyment. Every Bass worker was given their day's wages, plus extra spending money of a half-crown to a guinea – depending on their status within the company. Many chose to take up the option of bringing along their family members at a subsidised cost.

It was a massive undertaking and reputed to be the largest works' treat in the world. In order to make the most of the day the first train had left Burton at 3.50am. To allow workers who did not live in the town to join the trip, three trains began the journey from smaller local stations and two picked up in Derby.

As soon as the final train arrived, William Walters, who had been organising every detail of the trips since the beginning, sent a telegraph to Burton to let family and friends left behind know that everyone had arrived safely.

Special arrangements had to be made to house the trains in two miles of sidings. And because of the constant arrival of the Bass trains, some regular local services had to be delayed or rerouted.

The *Yarmouth Mercury* described the trip of 1901 to Great Yarmouth, noting that the sixteen trains required that year had taken sole use of the line from Burton to March, in Cambridgeshire, for several hours at the beginning and end of the day. Some trains running between Norwich and Great Yarmouth were cancelled entirely.

In general, however, resorts were only too happy for the boost to the local economy, particularly given that the brewer would prepay for its workers to enter many of the attractions. Bass also secured discounts on entry to a number of others.

The *Blackpool Herald & Fylde Advertiser* reported on the 1911 trip: 'Blackpool was invaded on Friday by 8,000 holidaymakers from Burton ... all the trains arrived in Blackpool about 1/4 of an hour before the scheduled time. The first battalion were here shortly after 7am and scores and scores had a refreshing early morning dip in the briny.'

William Walters always produced an illustrated brochure, some up to ninety-six pages long, which were handed to each day tripper and detailed all the attractions, places to eat, and additional outings and cruises that could be taken. The brochures also tended to include 'advice' on the importance of having a proper meal and other such 'helpful' information on travel etiquette, reminding passengers not to throw bottles from the train, or drop orange peel on the station platforms.

During the Edwardian years, the Bass railway trips alternated between Great Yarmouth, Scarborough, Blackpool and Liverpool – from which a free ferry ride could be taken to New Brighton. The last trip took place in July 1914, just a few weeks before the outbreak of war. As well as being a recreational and educational treat for workers, the trips were a potent advertisement for the company as newspapers up and down the country usually reported on the invasion of seaside resorts by brewery workers from a town far inland.

Britain's coastal towns did not, of course, rely solely upon the nation's industries to bring holidaymakers to them. By the beginning of the twentieth century towns like Blackpool were marketing themselves effectively in the nation's newspapers, supported by the railway companies that ran routes there. Brighton and South Coast Railway ran one in 1910 featuring a striking white cliff and golden beach, and the slogan 'Sea Breezes at the Sunny South'. Likewise, the Great Western Railway promoted its service to the 'Cornish Riviera'. Bournemouth was marketed as a year-round resort. The famous 'Skegness is so Bracing' posters, featuring the 'Jolly Fisherman', were first used by the London and North-Eastern Railways from 1908.

The Lincolnshire town of Skegness was generally regarded as a cheap and cheerful resort with its countless amusements and beach entertainment all targeting a mass market of working-class Britons. The Nottinghamshire Convalescent Home for Men had opened in 1891, and by 1907 several holiday camps and homes for poorer holidaymakers had been established there. Skegness, which has a very large beach at low tide, also boasted a pier complete with concert hall, saloon and a theatre. And there was also a fairground on the central beach with, from 1908, a roller coaster.

The modern perception of Blackpool is, perhaps, more one of kiss-me-quick hats and amusement arcades than of high culture. But the opening of Blackpool Tower in 1894, and its beautiful Tower Ballroom four years later, placed the town as the nation's firm favourite seaside resort. Particularly for those living in the industrial towns and cities of the North West – the tower could be seen from miles away.

The Bass excursion handbook of 1911 had described Blackpool Tower thus:

> Standing stately and stupendous at the very centre of the seafront, the most compelling landmark for many miles around, the tower may be looked for as the first sign of the end of our long journey. Soon after leaving Preston, if the weather is fine, we may expect to locate this monument of engineering skill, and, at its summit is brilliantly illuminated after dusk.

In 1896, a huge revolving wheel, some 250ft (76.2m) above the ground, had been attached to the tower. Until it was dismantled in 1928 as many as 900 people at a time were given a 16-minute long panoramic view of the town. With its three piers, Winter Gardens and

Pleasure Beach and horse-drawn trams, Blackpool had much to offer the visitor. As an advertisement in the *Graphic* of 23 May 1903 noted: 'See Blackpool and Live. Every taste gratified. Everything to please everybody. A wonderland by the waves. Easy of access from all parts. The children's paradise – firm golden sands. Safe boating and bathing. Mild and equable climate.'

The appeal of what would become Blackpool's Pleasure Beach, with its new American thrill rides like the Hotchkiss Bicycle Railroad Ride, Sir Hiram Maxim's Captive Flying Machine, the River Caves, the LaMarcus Adna Thompson's Scenic Railway, and William H. Strickler's Velvet Coaster, greatly enhanced its reputation. Blackpool council also made sure to advertise outside of the summer season. In October 1912 the town placed an advertisement in *The Sketch* noting: 'The question of the day is: Where shall we go for the Autumn Holidays? You will answer Blackpool, if you are wise. Because there is always something to amuse, somewhere to go at all times and in all weathers. Grand illumination of the Princess Parade. A Festival in Fairyland.' By the end of the Edwardian era, almost four million people arrived by train at one of Blackpool's then two railway stations each year.

Even taller than Blackpool Tower was New Brighton Tower. Opened in 1900, it was closed and dismantled in 1919 following a period of neglect during the First World War. The Wirral Peninsula town had grown steadily throughout the nineteenth century from a small settlement to a thriving commuter town and, eventually, a resort complete with pier, winter garden, theatres, and other amusements.

In contrast to the seaside resorts on the North-West coast, the small Norfolk seaside town of Cromer was regarded as an entirely more highbrow resort. Visitors there could expect an altogether more genteel experience. In its issue of 19 June 1901, society magazine *The Sketch* declared: 'This charming seaside resort has every attraction for people of the better class, and, with its new features, should draw many additional residents.'

From bathing huts pulled on to the beach, bathers could enter the water while guarding their modesty. Popular with rich Norfolk families and even royalty – Edward VII, as Prince of Wales, had played golf in the town, it was not immune to the latest crazes, however, and its elegant 151-metre-long pier, which dated from 1901, held roller skating sessions from 1907.

Further along the Norfolk coast was Great Yarmouth with its two piers. Wellington Pier dated from 1853 and was 210 metres long. In 1903 a disused cast-iron winter garden was shipped by barge from Torquay and installed next to the pier. Britannia Pier was opened in 1901 and is 40 metres longer than the older pier. Its first two pavilions (built in 1902 and 1910) were destroyed by fire – the second suffering a Suffragette arson attack. A third incarnation was completed in July 1914.

In the North East some port towns like Blyth, on the Northumberland coast, adapted to become seaside resorts. In the summer of 1905 local shop Smithson's – who had two branches in the town – ran a series of advertisements in the *Blyth News and Wansbeck Telegraph* for their 'enormous stock of spades, pails, shrimp nets, boats and ships from 1 pence'.

Seaside sundries were not only available in coastal towns. Liberty's in London's Regent Street could ensure that seaside-bound customers didn't arrive there empty-handed. According to a *Daily Mirror* advertisement of 7 August 1909, Liberty's had 'Seaside Toys ... moulds for sand pies in the shapes of dolls and goblets. A collection of delightfully amusing and pretty toys specially designed for children at the seaside and in country holiday resorts is obtainable.'

Brown, Muff & Co of Market Street, Bradford, was typical of stores that stocked bathing costumes, bathing tents, bathing chairs, tea baskets, trunks, straw hats and flannel suits.

In August 1901 the *Alfreton Journal*, a newspaper serving a Derbyshire town about as far from the coast as any other in Britain (Cleethorpes beach is around 65 miles – 104.6km – away), advised its readers to pack with care for their trips: 'It is well to remember that, though we may have a heatwave one day, it may be very different the next, and that it is always advisable to take a warm cape or coat for chilly evenings.'

Because the expanding railway network was the driving force behind the development of Britain's seaside towns, in addition to the attractive, enticing posters and snappy slogans, it was no surprise that the railway companies themselves seized upon the opportunity to establish as many services as they could from urban areas to the coast.

The Great Eastern Railway, for example, ran trains from London and its suburbs out to the Norfolk and Suffolk coast, and to the Essex resorts of Southend-on-Sea, Clacton-on-Sea and Harwich. A day trip to Clacton, from Liverpool Street or Stratford cost 4s 6d return.

Hoteliers, guesthouse owners and those with properties to rent out to holidaymakers were also keen to advertise. On a single day in 1909 the pages of the *Forest Hill & Sydenham Examiner* ran dozens of such listings. From 'a furnished cottage on the Isle of Wight close to the sea, very moderate terms', to the choice in Brighton, of the Haslemere Private Hotel 'fully licensed en pension [with all meals provided], separate tables', or the very comfortable apartments 'two minutes Palace Pier, close all amusements, pleasantly situated, good cooking', or even the 'homely' boarding establishment, opposite the West Pier.

Along the coast at Eastbourne were 'bedrooms and sitting rooms, very comfortable apartments, minutes from the sea, terms moderate, no children', while at Boscombe, 'furnished apartments for invalids and others' were available.

In Norfolk, options included Cromer apartments with 'sitting room, two airy bedrooms, terms moderate', the Cecil Boarding House in Great Yarmouth, 'facing sea, electric light throughout, every comfort', and a 'high-class board residence' at Gorleston-on-Sea.

In addition to such advertisements, newspapers provided reports, not just of the weather ('Blackpool very fine to showery, Bournemouth cloudless day, Skegness nine and a half hours' sunshine'), but also of the latest news from the resorts ('Margate – the town is overflowing with visitors who arrived at the weekend in phenomenal numbers by boat and rail.').

So popular were trips to the seaside that they became part of popular culture. In 1909, Mark Sheridan recorded John H. Glover-Kind's new music hall song *Oh, I Do Like To Be Beside The Seaside*. The version we are more familiar with today is that popularised by Reginald Dixon, the resident organist at the Tower Ballroom, Blackpool between 1930 and 1970, and is generally missing the four verses of the original.

For children, no visit to the seaside was complete without building a sandcastle and riding a donkey. Both traditions seem to have had their origins in the mid-nineteenth century. However, when it came to the latter, animal welfare had not proved particularly high on the list of priorities. By 1906, however, measures were being taken to protect the wellbeing of the gentle creatures.

Clacton Urban Council refused licences for donkey riding on its beach unless owners undertook to show no cruelty to the donkeys, as well as to promise there would be 'no bad language' on the part of the drivers or riders.

In 1914, Walter Betts, secretary of the Animal Hospital and Institute of Knightsbridge, wrote to *The Daily News* to complain about the lack of care given to donkeys:

> These little animals are treated with scant kindness and frequently with cruelty by their owners … The hours are often very long, and if business is lively the donkey is not given any rest or even time for food during the day. It would be an act of greatest charity to these unfortunate creatures if animal lovers residing in these resorts would first appeal to their owners, and, if unsuccessful, then to the local authorities, to enforce a rule that the animals should be unsaddled for an hour during the day and to see that they have proper food and water.

Some resorts went a step further than using donkeys and ponies, and offered large 'seaside goats', which were put to work pulling small carts loaded with children across the sands and along the promenades. And the goats seemed to fare even worse than the poor donkeys. A dedicated 'goat stand' was marked out on the road near Brighton's Palace Pier where the last known 'Harness Goat' licence was issued in 1953.

The last summer of the Edwardian era was that of 1914. Britons spending their precious holiday time at the seaside might well have looked out to sea to notice some of the Royal Navy's newest ships moored off the coast. They were not, as one might assume, deployed there to provide defence. Rather, they were there to show Britons just what their taxes had been spent on. Within weeks those ships would prove a vital part of the nation's fighting forces.

CHAPTER 14

The Holly and the Ivy

> Such objectionable practices as carol singing had been very much controlled, and the police deserved to be complimented.
>
> Alderman S Edwards,
> Chairman of the Bench,
> Aston Branch Police Court,
> 22 December 1913

At no time was an Edwardian home more welcoming than at Christmas. Fireplaces and bannisters were bedecked in lush natural greenery such as holly, ivy, yew, mistletoe and laurel taken from gardens and waysides.

Christmas trees had been a feature of a British family Christmas since they were introduced by the king's father, Prince Albert. And while there were commercial decorations in many shops, most trees – brought into the home on Christmas Eve – were adorned with simple home-made decorations like paper chains, ribbons and candles.

Shops and businesses took advantage of the increasingly widespread electricity supply to add a touch of twinkle to their decorations – and to the nation's high streets.

Electric Avenue in Brixton had been erected in 1888, with an iron and glass canopy installed across it shortly afterwards. It was reputedly the first shopping street in the country to be lit by electricity, and became renowned for its extravagant Christmas decorations, so much so that Londoners thronged to the street just to see them.

In 1908 the *South London Press* described the Christmas scene:

> The decorations here have been carried out almost entirely with natural evergreen. The entrance to the avenue is marked by a large illuminated crescent device in evergreen, bearing the words in electric letters 'A Merry Xmas'. Looking through the avenue one is astonished to see the thousands of coloured glow-lights hanging like strings of jewels from festoons of berry holly, conveying to one Christmas at every turn. A number of trees dotted with coloured lights form one of the most striking features of the decorations. In the centre of the avenue, suspended overhead, is a massive horseshow made entirely of laurel etc, edged with electric glow-lights, while carried from under are festoons of natural chrysanthemum blooms, the whole studded with coloured lights. Under this is a large crimson banner bearing the inscription 'To those who pass beneath this shoe a happy year will bring to you.'

A particularly popular aspect of the Christmas decorations that year, especially among excited children, were the enormous 'bon-bon' decorations that contained hundreds of small Christmas crackers that were periodically 'released'.

The first commercially produced Christmas card had been sold in 1843 and, by the Edwardian age, they had become a tradition. By 1913 companies specialising in them proliferated and, each year, cards were one of the earliest Christmas products to be advertised. Austin's Printing Works placed an advertisement in the *Faversham News* in mid-October reminding customers, 'Now is the time to order for Foreign and Colonial Mails.'

Popular among the well-to-do was the personalised Christmas card. Companies such as Orient produced sample books from which designs could be chosen. Some were fairly generic and rather non-seasonal, others bore monograms, or photographs. And there were even options suitable for use by families mourning a loved one. More Yuletide options featured sentimental scenes like a snowy churchyard or village, grazing deer, or a family gathered around a piano. There were sometimes as many as eight different greetings options from which to choose, with the option to have a family's or individual's name and address printed within the card.

Many chose to purchase cards off-the-shelf from local shops. The great Belfast department store of J. Robb & Co, on the corner of Castle Place and Lombard Street, offered the 'newest designs in Christmas cards … an endless variety to select from …'

According to the large advertisement it placed in the 20 December 1901 issue of the *Irish News And Belfast Morning News*, Robb's also offered an 'immense display of toys and fancy goods … an unlimited variety of articles for presents at prices to suit all classes of purchasers'. There, it claimed, every department was 'Replete With The Latest Novelties for the Season'.

Around the corner, on Donegall Place, was Langtry's store which advertised 'the very latest styles in high class neckwear – gentlemen's scarves, ties and mufflers, finest silks procurable, rich colourings, artistic designs.' The store also had a variety of 'Gloves! Gloves!! Gloves!!!' These varied from the more durable cape leather, to the softer suede and chevrette, and there was also a reindeer version, which was featured a 'natural hair lining'.

Other potential gifts were 'real lace' collars and handkerchiefs, umbrellas, and ladies' shirts and blouses in silk, cashmere and the still new Viyella, which was an almost equal blend of merino wool and cotton that had been patented in 1893. It was reputed to be the 'first branded fabric in the world'.

A short distance away, on Royal Avenue, E. McKenna & Co, manufacturing furrier, suggested that fur muffs would make ideal gifts for 'ladies, maids and children'. Mackenzie and McMullen's Scotch House (which occasionally described itself as a 'cheap drapery') on High Street, had its own 'Christmas Bazaar and Fancy Fair', and invited the public to 'a Free Promenade through the extensive premises to view the novelties.'

Not everyone in Edwardian society was fortunate enough to be able to afford, or expect to receive, lavish gifts. Fortunately, the notion of charitable giving was also enjoying a boom and there were many organisations willing to arrange treats for the poor. In 1901, in Manchester, this took several forms. Some 2,000 children from the Deansgate area were given toys and items of clothing by the Wood Street Mission. The Band of Kindness and Children's Help Society distributed 520 hampers to children 'confined to their home through sickness or infirmity' – containing all the seasonal treats they might otherwise have missed out on: a plum pudding, two mince pies, a meat pie, a variety of other comestibles' plus toys and a card or a letter. Manchester City Mission transformed the Free Trade Hall into a huge refectory catering for 2,500 'aged poor'. According to a report in the *Manchester City News*, 150 of them were 'totally blind, five were over 90 years of age, 68 were over 80, and 400 over 70 years of age', and each received a bag containing pies, meat and mince, a plum pudding, tea cakes, two ounces of tea and some sweets – some of which was intended to be consumed at home.

The Charter Street Ragged School opened its doors on Christmas morning for 1,600 poor local children who were fed breakfast, entertained and sent home with toys and dolls, sweets and oranges, a Christmas card and a penny.

This altruistic sentiment carried on right through the period. As did, for those who could budget for it, the festive feasting.

In December 1913, in the pages of the *Birmingham Daily Mail*, Lipton's advertised its 'stock of Xmas cheer'. Its famous tea was described as 'an acceptable gift', but there was plenty else to choose from to add to a family's Christmas meals. Lipton's Cocoa, priced fourpence-ha'pny per quarter pound tin, was described as 'nutritious and sustaining', and it was possible to collect special labels from large tins of cocoa which could be exchanged for 'a presentation box of finest quality chocolates' at any of the firm's branches. Lump sugar, 'Gold Medal' butter and margarine 'made from nuts and cream', 'Cambridge sausages' – a lightly spiced and herbed version of the popular food, – 'delicious breakfast bacon', a fine selection of the very best mild-cured hams and dried fruits were all on sale. As were plum puddings, mincemeat, jams, table jellies, cakes and shortbreads and, of course, the important poultry – 'turkeys, geese, ducks and fowls – finest quality obtainable'.

In Leicester, where that year's pantomime was *Sinbad the Sailor*, performed at the Royal Opera House, 'Havana, Mexican and British cigars … Virginian, Turkish and Egyptian cigarettes', 'Rest-Ur-Self Easy Chairs', as well as Crown Derby, Coalport and Royal Worcester porcelain, were touted as ideal presents by various shops in the town that would gain city status in 1919.

Visits to church, joining carol singers around the neighbourhood, or perhaps an evening of singing around the family piano, were all popular festive diversions. While most of the popular Christmas carols dated from Victorian times, or even earlier, two of what we still consider our most beloved carols have their origins in the Edwardian age.

In the Bleak Midwinter was based on a poem of the same name by Christina Rossetti, written in 1872. In 1906, British composer Gustav Holst put the words to music for the English Hymnal, while an alternative tune, more suitable for a seasoned choir, was written by Harold Darke in 1909.

The Holly and the Ivy was an older song featuring elements of pagan symbolism. It was published in 1911 by Cecil Sharp – a keen collector of English folk songs – who had 'discovered' it in Chipping Campden two years earlier.

CHAPTER 15

DEATH OF THE PEACEMAKER KING

> I am deeply grieved to inform you that my beloved father, the King, passed away at a quarter to twelve.
>
> King George V,
7 May 1910

On the early evening of 27 April 1910, the Prince of Wales, Prince Arthur of Connaught, Prime Minister H.H. Asquith and Home Secretary Winston Churchill, gathered at Victoria Station to welcome home King Edward VII from his trip to Biarritz, the French seaside resort so favoured by the rich and famous.

It was reported that the monarch had greatly enjoyed his time there, and that his health, which had been troubling him of late, had benefited greatly from the visit. In fact, Edward was suffering from severe bronchitis and his condition was about to take a turn for the worse.

A week later, Queen Alexandra and her daughter Princess Victoria, following a visit to the Queen's brother, George I of Greece, arrived in Dover aboard the Royal Yacht. When the King failed to meet his wife and daughter on their arrival at Victoria Station, and the royals were taken from there to Buckingham Palace with some haste, concerns were raised. And when the suggestion of a 'slight indisposition' failed to satisfy concerns for the monarch, the severity of the King's condition was made public. An official statement from his doctors revealed that Edward had been confined to his room for two days. Then came the first hint of a serious problem: 'His Majesty's condition causes some anxiety.'

The Liverpool Echo reported that the Queen 'went to His Majesty's room immediately on her arrival at the Palace, and spent a considerable time by his side'. Reports that the Prince of Wales had spent much of the past two days at his father's bedside came as something of a shock since, upon his return from the Continent, Edward had seemingly been able to continue his usual activities unaffected by his condition – he had attended the opera, met with the Prime Minister and with Lord Kitchener, and held a number of other audiences. He had even spent a weekend at Sandringham where – according to reports – although arriving at church by motor car, after the service he had walked back to the house.

But if newspaper readers needed the full level of concern for the royal patient spelling out, it surely came in the revelation that every part of Buckingham Palace was being kept as quiet as possible, to the point that carriageways under the arches at the front of the palace had been covered with peat to deaden the sound of the horses' hooves and the rattle of the carriage wheels. Later came word that there was now 'grave anxiety'.

On Friday, 6 May, thousands gathered outside Buckingham Palace, anxious for further news. *The Daily Mirror* reported:

> Policemen on duty round the gates had little trouble in keeping the large crowds in order. Everybody was subdued and people spoke to each other in whispers. Women jostled with the crowd with an absolute disregard for smart hats or frocks; stockbrokers and City men tore up in taxicabs and asked the nearest person the latest news.

As the 6.30pm bulletin was posted to the gates, one member of the public shouted for someone to read out the statement. No one did, and so each person had to file to the front to learn the gravest of news about their King. Then, 'a woman cried, "Oh, it cannot be! Oh God save his Majesty."'

All day a procession of dignitaries from archbishops to ambassadors, politicians to the nobility, had made their way to the palace. And now, all evening, members of the public made their way to the railings to read the bulletin, and many walked away wiping tears from their eyes.

Inside, the King suffered a number of heart attacks before losing consciousness around 11.30pm. He was taken to his bed where he lay surrounded by his family. Fifteen minutes later, Edward VII was dead. Shortly after midnight the news was posted to the palace gates.

The death of a second monarch in less than a decade came as a huge shock to the British people, even though Edward had been almost 60 years of age when he had inherited the throne. His reign had been a short one, but significant in terms of shaping life in Britain. He had succeeded in modernising the Royal Family. He had used his considerable charm, and his wide family network, to soothe international relations during a time of increasing tensions. These efforts had earned him the soubriquet 'Edward the Peacemaker'.

His patronage of the arts and of sports had helped to shape British leisure time. His people had grown accustomed to his being there – after all, they had watched on for almost sixty years as he served as Prince of Wales. They did not mind his playboy reputation – they saw a monarch who had extended the royal social circle to include a wide range of society, a king who had brought the monarchy and the people together by reintroducing the great public events his widowed mother had shied away from. Most importantly, they admired and loved Edward VII

While preparations were being made for the public funeral, at Queen Alexandra's insistence the body of the late king remained in his room. Only on 14 May, having been dressed in his uniform and his body placed in an oak coffin, was Edward moved to the throne room at Buckingham Palace where he lay in state for three days. Three days later he was taken to Westminster Hall which was, for the first time, used as the location for the public lying-in-state of a monarch, just as it had for William Gladstone three years earlier.

Over three days, half a million citizens filed past Edward VII's coffin. On the first day, when the gates closed at 10pm, an estimated 25,000 were turned away. So many members of the public queued that when his nephew, the German Kaiser, requested that the hall be closed while he privately laid a wreath, the police feared disorder, and so the Kaiser was taken in through another entrance while the public continued to file by. It was assumed that theatres and other places of entertainment would be closed during the lying-in-state, but the new King decreed that they should not, 'in view of the loss that would be inflicted on many persons ill able to bear it'.

The funeral, which took place on 20 May, was, of course, as grand as it was sombre. Although on this occasion the Duke of Norfolk, as Earl Marshall – the man responsible for ceremonies including coronations and state funerals – proved that organisational ability was not his greatest asset. On the evening before the service, courtiers had to rewrite the ceremonial directions, which were full of unhelpful errors – it was too late to correct those found in the printed order of service.

Nonetheless, it was the largest gathering of European royalty ever to take place. In addition, royal representatives from lands outside Europe included Egypt, Siam, China and Japan, as well as former US President Theodore Roosevelt, and the French Minister for Foreign Affairs, Stephen Pichon. Some 35,000 soldiers lined the procession which was watched by between three and five million members of the public. It was led by Caesar, the late King's dog, and travelled from Buckingham Palace to Paddington Station, where the cortege and mourners boarded the royal train, hauled by the steam locomotive King Edward, bound for Windsor. There a full state funeral was held at St George's Chapel, during which, for the first time at a monarch's funeral, the congregation sang two hymns.

Unlike his father, when it came to state affairs and what was expected of him, George V had long been well-informed. While Victoria had kept her son well away from her queenly duties, Edward had ensured that by the time his heir became king he would be experienced in the role. The pair had been very close, and, on the evening of Edward's death, George had written in his diary:

> I have lost my best friend and the best of fathers ... I never had a [cross] word with him in my life. I am heart-broken and overwhelmed with grief but God will help me in my

responsibilities and darling May will be my comfort as she has always been. May God give me strength and guidance in the heavy task which has fallen on me.

Like her father-in-law, 'May', as she was known within the family, was a great-grandchild of George III, although not herself descended from Queen Victoria. Despite her relatively non-royal background, she was ideally suited to marry into the British Royal Family. And, it seemed, she had been very much destined to become Queen Consort. Her first fiancé had been Edward's eldest son, Prince Albert Victor, Duke of Clarence and Avondale, known within the family as 'Eddy'. However, six weeks after their betrothal was announced the young prince died from influenza. The following year, she became engaged to his brother, Prince George, Duke of York. Upon their coronation, the new queen consort chose to use her second name 'Mary'. She was the first British queen consort to be born in Britain since Catherine Parr, the sixth wife of Henry VIII. George and Mary made a perfect team. They had eventually fallen deeply in love and were well-matched. George often consulted with his queen about matters of state business, and she would regularly contribute to his speeches. For his part George had long since carved his own path. As Prince and Princess of Wales, the couple had toured British India. George, in particular, had been appalled by the racial discrimination he witnessed and called for greater involvement for Indians in the governing of their own country. And as new monarch, he had refused to perform the state opening of parliament until a rather anti-Catholic passage of the Accession Declaration had been altered.

The coronation took place on 22 June 1911. After the issues encountered during Edward VII's funeral, the Duke of Norfolk remained only nominally in charge of proceedings – as chairman of the Coronation Executive Committee. Prime Minister Asquith insisted that the details be attended to by professional organisers employed by the Office of Works. The day itself was overcast and somewhat showery. As they were one of the few elements easily viewable by the general public, the processions to and from Westminster Abbey caused great excitement. Fourteen carriages transported representatives of foreign royal families and governments. Five state landaus carried members of the wider royal family. In the fifth of them rode the King and Queen's own children: the Prince of Wales (later Edward VIII), Princess Mary (later Princess Royal), Prince Albert (later George VI), Prince Henry (later Duke of Gloucester) and Prince George (later Duke of Kent).

Four carriages containing the officers of state followed before the spectacular Gold State Coach carrying the King and Queen. On the return from the Abbey, the processions took an extended route through Pall Mall, St James's, Piccadilly, and Constitution Hill. Some 45,000 troops either participated in the procession, or lined the route. The crowds were excited and celebrated wildly. Queen Mary wrote in her diary that they had received a 'magnificent reception both going and coming back'.

The new king noted that at times he had found it an emotional experience: 'I nearly broke down when dear David [the Prince of Wales] came to do homage to me, as it reminded me so much when I did the same thing to beloved Papa. He did it so well.'

Two days later the King and Queen attended a Coronation Review of the Fleet at Spithead. The new monarch was a keen supporter of the Royal Navy – indeed, until Eddy's death, he had seemed destined for a life-long service in it – and had encouraged a number of reforms. Close to a quarter of a million people watched from the shore as the royal couple, aboard HMY *Victoria and Albert*, reviewed some 167 Royal Navy warships, and eighteen others from foreign navies, stretched across five lines of six miles in length between Portsmouth and the Isle of Wight.

The final coronation spectacle did not take place until November 1911, when George and Mary became the only monarchs to attend their own Delhi Durbar. While Edward VII had felt a great attachment to Britain's European neighbours, George V, during his time as Prince of Wales on extensive overseas tours, had formed a strong affection for the British Empire. Although he took seriously the importance of a monarch remaining politically neutral at all times, George V is known to have been sympathetic to those campaigning for Indian independence and for Irish Home Rule. He was also aware, perhaps more than any monarch before him, that in order to remain a successful organisation in the future, the Empire needed to change. And he came to feel that he had been rather railroaded by Asquith over the Prime Minister's battle with the House of Lords when it came to passing radical legislation through the Upper House. He was determined this would not happen again.

There has been some suggestion that George V was guilty of inaction as the European Continent moved towards conflict come the summer of 1914. This is unfair. His constitutional powers were extremely limited, unlike those of his cousins, the German Kaiser and the Russian Tsar. Nonetheless, he endeavoured to caution against hostility and urged restraint, using the occasion of a family wedding – that of the Kaiser's daughter, Louise – to do so.

At just after half past eleven on the morning of 22 May 1913, George V stood alongside his cousin, Kaiser Wilhelm II, at Berlin's Anhalter Bahnhof – a beautiful railway station in the centre of Berlin, which served as the city's grand arrival point for all diplomatic and royal visitors. Opened by the Kaiser's father, and his chancellor, Otto von Bismarck, in 1880, it would become, for a time, Europe's largest railway station. The men were waiting for the Russian Imperial armoured train that was carrying another cousin – the Russian Tsar Nicholas II – from the frontier station at Eydtkuhnen [now Chernyshevskoye in Russia], then the eastern terminus of the Prussian railway.

Berlin, although gaily decorated for the celebrations, actually less favoured a family wedding than a political summit, thanks to the arrival of some 400 Russian secret service police who mingled with the crowds and watched over proceedings from Berlin's rooftops. London's *The Evening News* reported that, for the arrival of the Tsar, 'the area surrounding was converted for two hours into a police camp ... Wherever the eye wandered constables with Brownings [US-manufactured firearms] strapped menacingly to their belts filled the perspective.'

The Tsarina did not accompany her husband to Germany. Instead, the Tsar brought with him a number of attendants wearing white lambswool caps, as well as a several Russian priests. For the greeting, the Kaiser had chosen to wear the uniform of the Russian Grenadier Guard Regiment.

Reunited, the trio embraced each other warmly and moved to review the Guard of Honour together.

With both Tsar and King bearing a striking familial resemblance, the correspondent of the *New York Times* noted that it was, at times, difficult to tell the two men apart. Were it not for the fact that the men's uniforms were so different – the Tsar in the deep blue uniform of the Prussian Alexander Grenadier Guards, King George in the white uniform of the 8th Rhenish Cuirassiers, it was claimed it might have proved impossible, even for those who knew the men well.

The Tsar was taken to his accommodation while King George and Queen Mary spent the afternoon at the races in the Grunewald at the site earmarked for the ill-fated 1916 Olympic Games.

There was no rest for the Kaiser, however. It had already been a long day but he had more guests to greet. Generally accompanied by his wife and daughter and her husband-to-be, he had spent much of his time travelling to and from Anhalter Bahnhof to welcome various parties of family members. A waiting room had been set aside to allow the Kaiser to make repeated changes of uniform in between greetings.

On one occasion, according to the *New York Times*, the usually perfectly punctual Kaiser was late to greet one of the trains, and onlookers 'were treated to the spectacle of His Majesty in a hasty run endeavouring to reach the halting place of the railway car before his aunt [the Duchess of Baden] stepped out. He lost the race.'

It was not the only mishap that day. In the afternoon the Duke of Cumberland's car ran over a young boy outside the Charlottenburg Palace. The horrified Duke, 'sprang out' of his car and insisted on taking the lad to the hospital, where he was found to have only minor injuries.

The following summer, by which point the Continent was edging nearer to outright war. King George V found that his relationship with the Kaiser, which had always proved tricky, was faltering. As the nations prepared to square up to one another, silence fell between the rulers, and the pair would never speak again.

In hope that there was still time to intervene, George sent a personal message to his cousin, Nicky:

> I am most anxious not to miss any possibility of avoiding this terrible calamity which at present threatens the whole

world. I therefore make a personal appeal to you to remove the misapprehension which I feel must have occurred, and to leave still open grounds for negotiation and possible peace ... I will do everything in my power to assist ... I feel confident that you are as anxious as I am that all that is possible should be done to secure the peace of the world.

But it was too late. In reply the Tsar wrote: 'I would gladly have accepted your proposals had not German Ambassador this afternoon presented a note to my government declaring war ... Now that it has been forced on me, I trust that your country will not fail to support France and Russia. God bless and protect you.'

There was now nothing for George and Mary to do but to lead the country by example. By the end of the Great War only George, of the three cousins, retained his role. As the Edwardian era was brought to an end by war, it was too early for the nation to reflect that, throughout it, two kings and their queens had helped to redefine the relationship between monarch and people.

The modern era had begun ...

CHAPTER 16

THE LAST SUMMER

There are always clouds in the international sky. You never get a perfectly blue sky in foreign affairs. And there are clouds even now. But we feel confident that the common sense, the patience, the goodwill, the forbearance which enabled us to solve greater and more difficult and more urgent problems last year will enable us to pull through these difficulties at the present moment.

David Lloyd George,
17 July 1914

As ordinary a midsummer's day as any, 28 June 1914 was full of expectation of long, hot weeks to come. Most scheduled events had gone as planned with little interference from the weather. Attendees at the Derby, and Trooping the Colour had enjoyed particularly good conditions. The tennis at Wimbledon had begun in full sunshine. Now, as the tournament entered its second week, the newspapers reported that it was expected to continue in that vein.

According to reports in *The Globe*, the day saw an engineers' strike at Swansea which was affecting shipping at the port. In Haslemere, 'Mr Short' had discovered a young cuckoo in a wagtail's nest inside an oak tree. British motor car driver, Raphael C. Gimble, had been killed near Lyon when his car had overturned during automobile races. At Westminster, the Labour MP for Gorton, Mr John Hodge, a 'big and burly' man, had caused quite a stir in his 'coffee-coloured suiting of almost a muslin-like texture' – worn in contrast to the dark suits of almost everyone else in the chamber. And Derbyshire County Cricket Club were 233 all out in the second innings of their County Championship match against Somerset at the picturesque Queen's Park, Chesterfield. The match would prove a rare victory for the Derbyshire team in what would become an unfinished season.

Like so many aspects of British life, the so-called Golden Age of Cricket was about to come to an abrupt end because that late June day would become notable for something else. In the city of Sarajevo in the Austrian-annexed province of Bosnia, Archduke Franz Ferdinand, heir to the Austro-Hungarian throne, and his wife, Sophie, were both shot and killed by Gavrilo Princip. He was a student, and member of a Serbian nationalist organisation which sought Bosnian union with Serbia, thus ending Austro-Hungarian rule over Bosnia and Herzegovina. His actions were to cause a chain reaction that would bring Continental Europe to the brink of war.

The balance of peace in Europe had long been fragile. By 1914 Germany was the second most powerful economy in the world, and that nation's attempts at matching this with military might had raised suspicions and mistrust among its neighbours. Old established treaties saw Germany lined up with Austria-Hungary and the Ottoman Empire; and Russia with France and Britain – the Triple Entente. This was further complicated by Russia's alliance with Serbia, and Britain's promise to defend Belgian neutrality.

The assassinations had tipped the balance. Austria-Hungary sent Serbia a list of demands to which they could never agree. Germany, seeing an opportunity to drive a wedge between the Triple Entente, endorsed the ultimatum. While the Serbs did accept some terms, it was not enough and Austria-Hungary declared war. Germany warned Serbia's ally, Russia, not to mobilise in response and, for the next month, the situation would simmer away.

Westminster debated the unfolding political drama, and newspapers informed readers of the latest developments; for most Britons, however, life simply went on uninterrupted, for the time being at least.

On 1 July a report in the *Derby Daily Telegraph* noted that the regatta at Henley had begun. The attendance was down on previous years, but this had less to do with the international climate and more to do with the 'simply tropical' weather conditions. There were notably more international teams competing that year – with representatives from the United States, Canada, Italy and Ireland, as well as Belgium and Germany. Later in the day 'a dreadfully close and oppressive atmosphere' threatened a thunderstorm. The same could be said for the political situation on the Continent.

On 27 July the *Aberdeen Press & Journal* reported on a meeting at Steyning, Sussex, at which Francis Dyke Acland, Under-Secretary for Foreign Affairs, had talked of the 'cloud over Europe', and warned that 'no one could imagine the disasters a war – in which a great European Power was involved – might bring to the whole world'. It would not be long before they found out.

On 30 July Russia mobilised. Events now moved at lightning pace. Two days later Germany declared war on Russia, causing France to mobilise.

The *Stoke Sentinel* of 1 August 1914 outlined the complex situation and also considered the potential effects if Britain went to war. Already, local shopkeepers were feeling the effects of price increases on various common commodities. Britain relied heavily on imported goods. The wholesale price of sugar had already gone up 1s 4d per pound but was 'likely to go considerably higher'. There was also a possibility of 'scarcity owing to the fact that Germany and Austria are very large sugar supplying countries'. Austria had already banned the exportation of foodstuffs. Supplies of other foods like bacon, eggs and butter were also affected. A 'local tradesman' reassured that 'as long as we had command of the sea' the situation should not get too serious, particularly when it came to items imported from outside Europe, such as wheat. However, the same confidence did not extend to local manufacturers, where at least one pottery had reported cancelled orders from the Continent, and another warned that, in the event of war, it might have to shut down.

Monday 3 August was a bank holiday. With fear of imminent war came attempts by foreign investors to move their money away from Britain. At a time when it seemed that Britain would need plenty of money to fund its own war effort, the decision had been made to extend the bank holiday up to and including Thursday 6 August, creating the longest bank holiday in British history. It granted time for government and financial institutions to negotiate and pass essential legislation.

On 4 August, Germany turned its attention to France, demanding that Belgium permit German troops to pass through without resistance. Belgium refused, Germany declared war on France and invaded Belgium.

As the British government issued Germany with an ultimatum to withdraw from Belgium, the nation was living in a sort of duality between anticipating war and wishing to continue as normal. With a weather eye on developments, plans were still being made for the last weeks of summer.

Some citizens of Birmingham looked to their local newspaper for inspiration and made plans to visit Aston Reservoir Grounds Fun Park – 'Birmingham's New Pleasure Resort … beautiful lake surrounded by sylvan scenery, boats, pleasure craft, cycling on the water … and every Wednesday and Saturday "Brock's Great Crystal Palace Fireworks – most gorgeous displays ever seen in the Midlands"' – also band concerts twice daily and dancing all day. Demonstrations of Ju-Jitsu, side shows, a wild west show, sports and pastimes and a miniature railway.

At the Botanical Garden in Edgbaston there were 'conservatories, interesting displays of birds, animals and reptiles', and at the nearby Edgbaston Reservoir the 'Baskerville Prize Band, plus swimming exhibitions, rowing, sailing and motorboats'.

The Birmingham Athletic Institute alerted to its facilities the middle-aged, who could 'keep fit and well', and also the young, who could 'increase their height and build up a strong body'.

Hotels, guest houses and flats all across the country were still advertising their vacancies. For those seeking breaks closer to home, there was a daily bus service from the Bull Ring to Stratford upon Avon.

But there were many travelling that day who would rather not have been on the move. Thousands of military reservists, recalled to permanent service, were ordered to report immediately to their places of joining, without waiting for their individual call-up orders. Each reservist had a cash order in their identification papers which they could present at the nearest Post Office in return for three shillings in advance of pay. When they reached a transport hub, the railway or shipping company would issue each man with an appropriate ticket to travel. Territorials, too, had been told to be on standby for possible immediate deployment.

On the front page of the *Birmingham Mail* was an advertisement declaring 'War! War! War! All losses consequent upon war can be insured at Lloyds'. In contrast, and rather optimistically, immediately below this was another advertisement for daily boats from Harwich to the Hook of Holland and on to 'Holidays on the Rhine'. Also listed was travel agent Thomas Cook, which offered holidays and cruises in Britain and abroad. To 'Norway, Iceland, the Baltic, Russia, Germany, France, Belgium, Spain, Portugal, Madeira and Canaries'. Belgian State Railways even got in on the act. For many, however, that trip to the Continent was about to be made compulsory.

At just before midnight the Foreign Office issued a statement:

> Owing to the summary rejection by the German government of the request made by His Majesty's Government for the assurance that the neutrality of Belgium will be respected, His Majesty's Ambassador at Berlin has received his passport. His Majesty's Government has declared to the German government that a state of war exists between Great Britain and Germany as from 11pm on August 4th.

A strange mood pervaded the nation as it awoke on the morning of the 5th. Those who had been enthusiastic for war now had a cause around which to coalesce, and most of those who had urged caution now accepted the moral obligation in which Britain found itself.

On 9 August 1914, George V sent a message to his troops bound for the Continent which ended with the words: 'I pray God to bless you and guard you and bring you back victorious.'

Three days later Britain declared war on Austria-Hungary and a heady mix of patriotism and excitement began to bubble up.

The nation gathered itself for what lay ahead. The Golden Age had melted away.

INDEX

Abbey, Edwin Austin 35
Acland, Sir Francis Dyke 185
Adair, Eleanor (see Huntley
　Nicholson, Mrs Eleanor)
Adelina, Miss 155
Aked, Charles 30
Alexanders, George 154
Allan, Maud 136
Amundsen, Roald 88
Andersson, Mauritz 142
Archduke Franz Ferdinand 184
Arden, Elizabeth 124
Ashton, Miss Margaret 75
Asquith, Herbert Henry 50, 51, 53,
　62, 63, 67, 71, 87, 174, 178, 180
Astor, John Jacob 90
Atkinson, Mr J.B. 96

Baden-Powell, Robert 82
Baker, Lizzie 71
Balfour, Arthur 3, 48-50, 54
Ball, Lilian 67
Barker, Will 150
Barlow, Sir Thomas 38
Barnett, Dame Henrietta 108
Barrie, J.M. 152
Baxter, Mrs John 98
Beadon Woodforde, Colonel W. 69

Beck, Emma 12
Beerbohm Tree, Sir Herbert 152-153
Beeton, Isabel 120
Beeton, Samuel Orchart 120
Bell, Alexander Graham 112
Bentham, Dr Ethel 105
Bernhardt, Sarah 154
Billinghurst, Rosa May 63
Birkenhead, Earl of (see Smith F.E.)
Bleriot, Louis 133
Bodley, J.E.C. 41
Booth, Hubert Cecil 111
Booth, Walter R. 150
Bogannys, The 156
Brailsford, Henry 64, 66
Bright, Mrs Allan 57
Brockway, Fenner 93, 94
Brown, John 5
Buckingham, Mr H. 69
Burnett, Frances Hodgson 152

Campbell, Mrs Patrick 153
Campbell-Bannerman, Henry 50,
　59, 62
Capper, Mabel 71
Cassell, John Henry 110
Chamberlain Arthur 72
Chamberlain, Joseph 26, 27

Index

Champion, Harry 158
Chaplin, Charlie 156
Chirgwin, George 156
Churchill, Winston 52, 62, 63, 64, 66, 70, 174
Clarke, Mary 64
Clifford, Camille 130
Clifton, Herbert 148
Conan-Doyle, Sir Arthur 24, 29, 151
Cooper, Gladys 119
Crippen, Cora 84
Crippen, Hawley Harvey 83-86
Crown Princess of Sweden 137
Curtis-Bennett, Sir Henry 71
Curzon, Lord 11, 12, 178

Davenport, William 97
Davidson, Randall, Bishop of Winchester 44
Davison, Emily 76-78
de Coubertin, Baron Pierre 135
de Courcy Laffan, Reverend Robert Stuart 135
De Moleyns, Clara E. 128
Derby, Lord 62
Desborough, Lord 135-136
Dew, Chief Inspector Walter 84
Dewar, Captain David 82-83
Dickens, Charles 2
Dod, Annie 144
Dod, Charlotte 'Lottie' 144
Dod, Tony 144
Dod, William 144
Douglas, Johnny 143
Doxey, Anthony 98
Duchess of Connaught 137
Duff, Lady Alexandra 42
Duke of Cambridge 42
Duke of Connaught 2, 3, 11, 20, 42, 137

Duke of Cumberland 181
Duke of Norfolk 38, 177
Duke of York 3

Earle, Fred 154
Edwards, George 154
Edwards, Alderman S. 169
Elen, Gus 158
Elliott, Gertrude 153, 154
Elmore Belle (see Crippen, Cora)
Elsie, Lily 119
Endsor, Mr E. 69
Escoffier, Auguste 114
Evans, Gladys 71
Ewry, Ray 141

Fawcett, Henry 57
Fawcett, Millicent 29, 31, 56, 57, 61, 75
Fealy, Maude 119
Fields, Fanny 156
Fitzsimons, Mr & Mrs Bob 155
Fleming, Margaret 87
Forbes-Robertson, Johnstone 153, 154
Ford, Florrie 158
Forster, E.M. 151
Forsythe, Fanny 123
Francis, Maudie 154
Fuller, Bampfylde 12
Funk, Casimir 113

Galsworthy, John 151
Gammon, Barclay 156
Garnett, Theresa 70
Garrett Anderson, Dr Elizabeth 56, 63
Garton, Frederick Gibson 117
Gibson, Charles Dana 129-130
Gimble, Raphael C. 183

Gladstone, Herbert 76
Gladstone, William 54, 76, 176
Graham, Florence (see Arden, Elizabeth)
Grahame, Kenneth 152
Green, Alice 77
Gruber, Max 155
Guggenheim, Benjamin 90

Hackenschmidt, George 150
Haggar, William 150
Haggard, H. Rider 151
Hall, Catherine 129
Halswelle, Wyndham 140
Hands, Charles E. 59
Hardie, Keir 60
Harmsworth, Alfred 107
Harmsworth, Harold 107
Harmsworth, St John 116
Harcourt, Sir William 52
Harris, Dr 96
Hart, Leolyn G. 117
Hawthorne, Lil 84
Hayes, Johnny 140
Hemming, Mrs (see Forsythe, Fanny)
Henderson, Henry 117
Hepworth, Cecil 150
Hewitt, David 46
Hicks, Thomas 139
Hobbs, Billy 154
Hobhouse, Emily 27-29, 34
Hodge, John 183
Holst, Gustav 20, 173
Hooley, Edgar Purnell 110
Hopkins, Mr 69
Houghton, Frederick 98
Howard, Sir Ebenezer 108
Hubbell, Harvey 111
Hume, Captain Arthur 29
Huntley Nicholson, Mrs Eleanor 123

Irving, Sir Henry 153
Ismay, Bruce 90

Jones, Bertie 78

Kaiser Wilhelm II 2, 177, 180, 181
Katos Komikal Kidgets 155
Kendall, Captain, Henry 85
King Alfonso XIII of Spain 148
King Edward VII 3, 7, 8, 10, 11, 17, 23, 31, 34, 35, 38, 40, 44, 70, 137, 139, 143, 148, 154, 165, 174, 176
King George V, 11, 17, 53, 55, 77, 155, 174, 175, 178, 179, 181, 182, 187
Kipling, Rudyard 152
Kirk, Richard 115
Kitchener, General Horatio Herbert 27, 31, 175
Kitson, Charles 154

Laking, Sir Francis 38-39
Lal Dhingra, Madan 12
Lalcaca, Dr Cawas 12-13
Lambert, Florence 147
Langtry, Lillie 153
Lascelles, Frank 20
Lashwood, George 147
Lauder, Harry 156
Layland-Barratt, Sir Francis 76
Lehar, Franz 119, 154
Leigh, Mary 71
Lemon, Etta 129
Leno, Dan 157
Lewis, Rosa 114
Liebig, Justus 116-117
Lloyd, Marie 146, 158, 159
Lloyd George, David 26, 47, 50, 51, 52, 62, 72-74, 183
Lonsdale, Lord 22

Index

Lorz, Frederick 139-140
Luck, Charles 109
Luck, Mary Ann 109
Lumiere Brothers 148

McAdam, John Loudon 110
McKenna, Reginald 71, 75
Mackworth, Captain Humphrey 72
Mackworth, Margaret 71-72
Mailes, Charles 147
Marshall, Catherine E. 75
Marshall, Emily 67
Martensson, Frithiof 142
Martin, Harry 22
Méliès, George 44-45
Michelham, Lady 143
Michelham, Lord 143
Milner, Alfred 27
Molyneux, Thomas 98
Moore, James 96
Morandinis, The Three 159
Morgan, Gwennie 155
Morley, John 30
Morris, Barry 155

Nash, John 84
Nesbitt, Edith 152
Nesbitt, Evelyn 130
Nethersole, Miss Olga 153
Netty Janowsky, The Four 155
Northcliffe, Lord (see
    Harmsworth, Alfred)

Pankhurst, Adela 58
Pankhurst, Christabel 62, 79, 133
Pankhurst, Emmeline 56, 58, 61,
    64, 79
Pankhurst, Mary 64
Pankhurst, Sylvia 63, 79
Parker, Barry 109

Parry, Hubert 20, 44
Paul, Robert 148
Palace Girls 156
Pavlova, Anna 156
Paxton, Joseph 17
Pelham-Clinton, Lord Edward 45
Pember Reeves, Maud 105
Penhaligon, William 125
Pern, Dr Norman 29
Perrier, Dr Louis 116
Pethick-Lawrence, Emmeline 58
Phillips, Eliza 129
Pichon, Stephen 177
Pietri, Dorando 140, 142-43
Poland, Hannah 129
Potter, Beatrix 152
Primrose, Dame Deborah 124
Prince Albert 2, 4, 169
Prince Andrew of Greece 42
Prince Arthur 2, 11, 42, 174
Prince George of Greece 42
Prince of Wales 2, 6, 36, 37, 39,
    45, 136, 137, 140, 174, 175, 176,
    178, 179
Princess Alice of Albany, Countess
    of Athlone 7
Princess of Battenberg 42
Princess Beatrice 45
Princess Frederica of Hanover 42
Princess Louise 42
Princess Sophia Duleep Singh 63
Princess Maud 42
Princess Victoria 42, 137, 148
Princip, Gavrilo 184

Queen Alexandra 37, 38, 45, 78,
    125, 174, 176
Queen Mary 155, 157, 178, 181, 182
Queen Victoria 1-7, 11, 35, 36, 63,
    80, 112, 128, 143, 177, 178

Ray, Elsie 159
Rea, Hope 57
Reid, Sir James 4
Rippon, William 125-126
Roberts, Lord 42
Robbins, William 140
Robey, George 156
Robinson, Robert 147
Rogan, Lt Dr J. MacKenzie 19
Roosevelt, Alice 139
Roosevelt, Theodore 177
Rose, Ralph 138
Rosebery, Lord 52
Rothermere, Lord (see Harmsworth, Harold)
Rothes, Countess of 90
Rover, Alf 159
Rubinstein, Helena 124

Salisbury, Lord 27, 47-48
Salisbury, Marquess of 3
Scott, Captain Robert Falcon 88
Selfridge, Harry Gordon 131-133
Semon, Sir Felix 37
Shaw, Edward 91, 95
Shaw, George Bernard 60, 152
Smith, F.E. 86
Sophie, Duchess of Hohenberg 184
Spilsbury, Bernard 86
Spooner, Reginald Herbert 143-144
Stead, William T. 44
Stern, Sir Herbert (see Michelham, Lord)
Stow, Percy 150
Sumner, John Jr 115-116
Swahn, Oscar 141

Temple, Frederick, Archbishop of Canterbury 45
Thayer, John 87-88
Tiller, John 156
Tilley, Vesta 157
Treves, Sir Frederick 39
Tuke, Mabel 67
Turton, William 98
Tyldesley, Mrs Miriam 98

Unwin, Raymond 109

Vanderbilt, Cornelius 136
Villiers, Edward Hyde, 5th Earl of Clarendon 3
Von Bismarck, Otto 180

Wallace-Dunlop, Marion 61
Walters, William 162
Webb, Sir Aston 20
Wells, H.G. 60, 151
Whitaker, Reverend John Ayton 69
Whitty, Frank 65
Williams, Henria Leech 64-65
Williams, Kate 'Vulcana' 84
Williams, Llewellyn 85
Williams, Ralph Vaughan 20
Williamson, Emily 129
Wilson, Alice 67
Windrum, Rhoda 154
Winstone, James 93
Woodiwiss, Alderman Abraham 40
Woodward, Bert 154
Wright, Wilbur 154
Wrighton, Norman 154
Wyllie, Sir Curzon 12-13
Wyllie, Lady 13